PRAISE FOR *MANAGING EMPLOYEE BURNOUT*

D1590877

'If you're a remote leader, *Managing Employee Burnout* is a must-have resource to identify, qualify and remedy your team members that are at risk of burning out before they do.'
Liam Martin, Co-founder, Running Remote and co-author of *Running Remote*

'A critical and much-needed resource for any CEO, leader or remote worker. This book gives us all the practical tips to finally create stress-free teams in a distributed environment.'
Nazim Ahmed, CEO, remx

'This is not just support for professionals and leaders; this guidebook is a resource that will turn your organization into a sustainable, high-performing and human-focused culture!'
Tony Jamous, CEO, Oyster

'Shauna Moran's book is practical, logical and well written, because she has been through this process herself and is therefore speaking from hard-earned experience. She writes in an accessible and understandable way. This is the way that the world is moving, so it makes sense to read this book and absorb its insights, so that you can retain and inspire your own workforce.'
Simon Cocking, Irish Tech News

'In this world of constant remote working, employee wellness and burnout should be a priority for all organizations. This book is filled with great tools and practical strategies for getting remote work right!'
Brian Scudamore, Founder and CEO, O2E Brands and author of *BYOB: Build your own business, be your own boss*

'Shauna Moran is a true professional and one of the few experts in the field of remote work that has the longstanding experience and knowledge base to help companies and individuals of all shapes and sizes as they navigate the sometimes-challenging waters of distributed teamwork. Her work at Operate Remote speaks for itself, and this book is just one more example of how she is pushing the future of work forward.'
Chase Warrington, Head of Remote, Doist

'Finally, a real business how-to for how we can all reduce unhealthy stress within our workplace. Shauna Moran shows you how to create a sustainable culture and find efficiencies in running your team in a distributed way, so we can enjoy the work again.'
Job van der Voort, CEO, Remote

Managing Employee Burnout

*How to develop a happy, healthy
and engaged workforce*

Shauna Moran

KoganPage

Publisher's note
Every possible effort has been made to ensure that the information contained in this book is accurate at the time of going to press, and the publishers and author cannot accept responsibility for any errors or omissions, however caused. No responsibility for loss or damage occasioned to any person acting, or refraining from action, as a result of the material in this publication can be accepted by the editor, the publisher or the author.

First published in Great Britain and the United States in 2023 by Kogan Page Limited

2nd Floor, 45 Gee Street	8 W 38th Street, Suite 902	4737/23 Ansari Road
London	New York, NY 10018	Daryaganj
EC1V 3RS	USA	New Delhi 110002
United Kingdom		India

www.koganpage.com

Kogan Page books are printed on paper from sustainable forests.

ISBNs
Hardback   978 1 3986 0809 2
Paperback   978 1 3986 0807 8
Ebook   978 1 3986 0808 5

British Library Cataloguing-in-Publication Data
A CIP record for this book is available from the British Library.

Library of Congress Cataloging-in-Publication Data
[to follow]

Typeset by Integra Software Services, Pondicherry
Print production managed by Jellyfish
Printed and bound by CPI Group (UK) Ltd, Croydon, CR0 4YY

CONTENTS

ABOUT THE AUTHOR

Shauna Moran is a remote and hybrid team workplace expert, international public speaker and author. Her award-winning executive coaching agency, Operate Remote, empowers leaders and their remote teams to create and build more emotionally healthy, engaged and sustainable organizations so they can scale and grow with confidence, regardless of locations.

Shauna began academically researching remote teams over six years ago when she was a leader in a hybrid environment. The challenges she and her team faced propelled her to uncover the most sustainable and effective strategies for building highly functional remote-first organizations.

With a background in psychology, Shauna knew that it wasn't just processes and strategies that teams needed to be successful remotely – it was in fact a mindset shift. Shauna then decided to qualify as an executive coach. Today, she blends both remote-first processes and strategies with the psychology of leading remote teams to ensure teams are set up not only to work remotely but to thrive in remote and hybrid environments.

From working with dozens of organizations like Webflow, Infinera, O2E Brands, Shell International, Enterprise Ireland, Shopify, and many more all over the world, Operate Remote has been recognized as one of the Top Leadership Training and Coaching Businesses in Europe for 2020.

Shauna currently resides in Vancouver, British Columbia (on the unceded territories of the Musqueam, Squamish, or Tsleil-Waututh nations) with her partner David and dog John. You can read more about Shauna and her work by visiting www.operateremote.com.

PART ONE

The Self

1

Introduction to burnout: my story

It was a game-changer for me, not having to commute a long distance to work every day. My excitement and anticipation for working from my own home grew as I approached my first day working from my downstairs office.

I had everything I needed: my laptop, two screens, my office set up with all the mod-cons and a dog bed for my springer spaniel, Ruby. The week before, I went shopping for new slippers and cosy jumpers and trousers – after all, I didn't have to think about what I needed to wear anymore. Or did I?

About two months into my remote position, the initial excitement of working from home started to wear off. I was passionate about my work, performing well and feeling like a part of a team, but something in my day-to-day life just felt off. I noticed that I didn't feel like myself – I was fatigued, unmotivated and generally low in my mood. I struggled to switch off from work and I felt like my weeks were just one big blur of computers, screens and Slack notifications. Instead of spending my mornings doing self-care (like I had planned), I was struggling to get out of bed and crawling my way into my office at 8 am.

What had changed, I wondered?

Looking back now with the experience and insight I have, it's clear that I had suffered a mild burnout. This burnout was caused by my lack of self-awareness of my own needs (which I'll cover later in the book). I was young, hungry to make a difference in my workplace and not fully aware of what I needed to do (or not do) to feel good in myself. I viewed productivity as a linear process back then, and I thought I needed to 'just keep working' to achieve my work goals. I failed to see what elements contributed to my personal productivity levels.

I hadn't developed my emotional intelligence to a stage where I could identify the habits and practices that I needed each day to maintain wellbeing while working from home.

It wasn't until I reflected on my life outside the house that the light-bulb went on. I calculated that I had not left the house at all during my working week. That's right – no meetups with friends, no hobbies or activities or even exercise classes. I had barely got outside for fresh air.

While you might not be shocked to hear about this experience, considering how the remote work landscape has been since the 2020 pandemic, reflecting on the extent to which my mental health was suffering is eye-opening. Some of you might relate to my experience. Some of you might have had a lightbulb moment when reading this or witnessed this particular type of burnout in your team members.

You see, as remote workers, we have to take responsibility for our own wellbeing. Through the years, in focusing on my working habits and helping others with theirs, I've realized that finding out what works for us as unique human beings requires experimentation.

Experimentation is precisely what I started to do.

I experimented with getting dressed every day and feeling good in my appearance and noted how that impacted my mood. I experimented with getting outside for a walk for fresh air before and after work and noted how that influenced my mental wellbeing. I scheduled a couple of activities each week outside the house to meet friends and connect with people. With this experimentation, I started to witness a change in myself. I was more energized, generally happier and even more motivated at work. Over time, and with an open mind, I had finally found ways to navigate the burnout that came from a lack of self-awareness as a remote worker. However, I wish that I had been educated and empowered to understand the risks that come with working from home for the very first time.

A second burnout

Little did I know it wouldn't be the last time I experienced burnout. Several years after working remotely in a different position, I experienced my second burnout. The position allowed me to travel globally, interact with clients around the world and work on a team of international colleagues. While this was great, it introduced global time zones and pressure to perform. Our team was essentially a startup within a multinational organization. It was a lot of fun, we learned a lot and we constantly experimented with strategies, trying to figure out what exactly worked. On the outside, it looked like the perfect job: travel, fun, impactful projects, and working with a diverse group of people based all around the world. On the inside, however, something else was true. It wasn't a healthy, sustainable working environment.

Constantly, I'd see my colleagues working late into the night to finish projects and taking on extra work. Our passion for what we did was nothing short of enormous, and that fed into unhealthy habits that we developed as a team. Leadership rewarded these unhealthy habits and encouraged team practices that didn't account for the importance of time away from work. I'd receive emails and messages from leaders on Sundays because they were 'just getting a new idea off the ground' and the pressure to perform outside the norm was created and accepted over time. Of course, you have to remain flexible when working on an international team. Taking calls at 5 am to accommodate time zones once a week is okay, but when you're also expected to take another call at 6 pm that evening, problems can arise. I could see the impact that constant overworking had on my team and our wellbeing.

As I'm describing here, the 'hustle' culture is solely focused on doing and executing, and is essentially a 'Go-Go-Go' mindset. It never takes a break. Combining this hustle culture with a team of intelligent, passionate and creative people without the guidance of leadership that promotes wellness and sustainability is risky. This type of culture doesn't recognize the importance of downtime, deep work (uninterrupted time to work without distractions), or reflecting before or after action.

This fun, high-achieving but unstainable environment eventually led to another burnout for me.

This burnout was a lot more severe for me personally. I experienced heightened emotions about the smallest things to do with my work. I was unable to think logically and was crippled with self-doubt and worry that I wasn't performing well enough. I feared I was letting my team down if I couldn't keep up with the unrealistic working practices. No matter how many vacation days I took or self-care practices I implemented, I just couldn't get back to feeling well and happy. I felt incredibly stuck and confused.

Of course, it's easy to look back now and see the type of burnout I experienced and the root causes behind it. This burnout was primarily caused by an unsustainable working culture within my organization, and I realized that there was little I could do to change that. No matter what I tried to change in my own life and work, I would always be met with an unhealthy team culture that didn't fully support or recognize my healthy boundaries.

Again, this is a situation I see time and time again when coaching and working with individuals that crave a healthier work environment. Sometimes, the culture is just so unhealthy that no amount of changes made by any one individual will make a difference in the long term. The change needs to happen from the top down, and if the top of the organization isn't comprised of emotionally intelligent, self-aware leaders, then it's unlikely that the culture will genuinely change.

Knowledge is power

At this time, I decided to go back to university while working full-time to research innovation management and base all of my research around remote working. For me, knowledge was power and if I could be empowered with what it takes to sustainably succeed as a remote team and worker, I could help my organization change for the better. In my research, I learned so much about remote leadership, cultures and teams. I discovered the core foundations needed to succeed in this new virtual world and was able to apply some of these practices and principles within my team to make a change for the better.

Of course, I had to experience yet another type of burnout to round out my story. This time, the root cause was professional unfulfilment and lack of role clarity. I was working for a startup company as a senior leader of their partnerships department. I had finally achieved what I considered to be my definition of success: salary, responsibility and a ton of opportunity for growth. After some time, however, I started to witness a personal struggle to 'keep going' and 'get on with work'. Priorities were constantly changing, as were the metrics and focuses we had as an organization. I'm all in when it comes to thriving on change, but when change was happening on a daily basis, I struggled to understand what exactly was expected of me and my team. I was challenged to find the motivation every day in my work and wondered why I felt so unhappy when I thought I had achieved exactly what I wanted in my career. At that time, I decided to pursue a new course in life and executive coaching and discovered the importance of personal values in creating a life of fulfilment. When I reflected on my values and my personal definition of success, I realized exactly why I was unfulfilled with my work. So many of my values were not reflected in my current definition of success and I had to redefine what success looked like to me at that stage in my life. The lack of role clarity was also something that greatly impacted my ability to feel secure and content in my job. I'm truly grateful for that stage in my career. It was indeed a pivotal moment that led me to create my own coaching and consultancy business, Operate Remote.

Today, as a remote and hybrid team performance coach, I work with organizations, teams and leaders to help them create engaging, productive and sustainable places to work. To help teams thrive in a remote environment, I help them build the internal processes that support them in making their work more efficient and effective. Of course, what is equally as important, but not as straightforward, is helping teams adapt their culture and their mindsets so that they can build working environments that are emotionally well and sustainable.

It was within the shift to remote working due to the 2020 pandemic that my focus became very clear. Every single company I spoke to had the same enormous blocker – their teams were burnt out, stressed and overwhelmed. Time and time again, I'd have conversations with leaders who were seeking answers on what to do next. Of course, the answers were never as simple as 'here is a one-size-fits-all answer that will immediately solve your team's burnout'. If companies really wanted to solve the burnout epidemic in their teams, they had to face and look at the truth – the root causes as to why their teams were experiencing this heightened stress. Similar to going to therapy, in order to emerge with a new perspective and strategies to manage emotional and mental wellbeing, a company had to be willing to be committed to understanding why. Some organizations want to address the problem by ticking a box – updating wellness perks or offering extra vacation time. As you'll discover later on in the book, ticking boxes doesn't make a difference in the long term. In fact, it rarely even works short-term. To truly reduce burnout in our teams once and for all, we need to be willing to be uncomfortable and take ownership as an organization and as leaders. This book is an opportunity for you to dig deep into the burnout issues you, your team or even your wider organization have been experiencing.

This book, the stories and research I share, will help you understand the different types of burnout that we experience in our working worlds and how the root causes of burnout can themselves have various root causes. With this important and ever-changing topic, it's never a one-size-fits-all solution because we are operating in a world of perspectives, individuality, personal experiences and values. I encourage you to work through the exercises included at the end of each chapter to get the most out of your investment in this book and to support you in understanding how these key concepts might apply to your team and organization. Remember, we're covering a wide range of experiences, perspectives and root causes of burnout; some might be applicable to you, some may not. Some might be applicable right now and others might be beneficial for you to understand in the future. Thank you for joining me on this journey and for committing to managing and reducing burnout once and for all. You are a big part of the solution – please don't ever doubt that.

Lessons about burnout

#1 Experiencing burnout has nothing to do with your strength of character

We've come a long way when it comes to talking about mental health on a global scale, thankfully. We do, however, still attach a stigma to people who experience burnout. It's like our subconscious is programmed to question the strength of someone's character and ability to do their job effectively if they experience mental health challenges or even a burnout. This book is all about the unfolding of burnout to help us realize that this challenge that many of us have experienced, or will experience, has absolutely nothing to do with how strong a person we are or how capable we are in our jobs and life. This is a really important one for us to remember. I know this deeply because I work with some of the most inspiring, strong and brilliant professionals day in, day out. They open up to me because I'm a qualified executive coach who creates vulnerable spaces for reflection and growth. Our biggest fear is often what people will think of us, which I believe prevents many individuals from finding solutions and support early on in the stress cycle. Through the stories I share in this book, my own and others', I hope to change how we see the person behind the burnout and thus create an environment where people feel safe, heard and fully supported.

#2 Burnout is rarely the result of one specific problem, but rather a combination of many

It's very rare that I've come across an individual who can exactly pinpoint the reasons and causes for them experiencing burnout. Sometimes I'll hear reflections like, 'I should have taken more time off in between changing jobs', and those cases can be easier to learn from. Most often and what's most common is that burnout rarely has just one cause. It's often a combination of many issues stemming from a lack of ownership of oneself, ineffective team processes and cultures, or even a lack of leadership. This is why I've created three sections within this book – The Self, The Organization and The Leader – so that we can identify the big B's (big burnout causes) and the little B's (smaller burnout causes) and paint a full picture as to why someone or a team experiences these challenges.

#3 Prioritizing oneself usually becomes non-negotiable after having experienced heightened stress

In my own experience, after each burnout experience, I took my self-care and wellbeing more seriously each time. Sometimes, we have to go through it to understand the importance of a lesson. Often, we'll continue to experience the same problem over and over again until we learn the lesson. The journey of life. While the lesson doesn't appear when you're in the problem, when the dark night passes and the sun rises again, we can start to see the meaning behind our experiences and learn more about ourselves, our needs and what's really important. Some of the most transformational leaders I've worked with in this space, those who support their teams and strive for emotionally and mentally healthy teams, have indeed experienced the pain of burning out themselves. Never underestimate how your story and experiences will help people in the future but remember, the lessons are for you first.

#4 Many people aren't willing to hold space for conversations about burnout

This one is even difficult to write about but it's true and it's really important. If you're reading this book, you're likely either experiencing heightened stress on your team or yourself or you want to prevent burnout from happening in the future. Reading this book is one of the first steps on that journey but how many of you are willing to openly have these conversations with people that you work with? Many people are uncomfortable with talking about burnout, stress and what it takes to create healthy teams in a professional environment. That discomfort is what is feeding this problem and causing it to never end in some cultures. It's not that we expect every professional to fulfil the role of a great therapist; let's leave that important work to the experts. We do, however, want to hold space and to create safety for the people we work with to speak up when they need to. If more people feel safe to do this, we are better able to manage this problem and nip it in the bud before people have to really suffer. In holding space, we don't necessarily have to have all of the answers, but we can be the supportive listener that helps remove the stigma and fear and gently navigate our colleagues towards hope, resources and a brighter future.

#5 Having conversations about preventing and managing burnout dissolves the isolation people feel and can be a healing modality in itself

In my work, I've found bringing groups of people together to spend time checking in with themselves and sharing their experiences with each other to be healing in itself. Often in remote team environments when we are isolated and physically separated from our colleagues we think that 'I'm the only person experiencing this'. We become protective and secretive of our stress, thinking that we're the only person within our team or organization who feels this way. This type of isolation can be a very lonely place and can only exacerbate the challenges we're experiencing. When teams come together to openly share, we hear comments like 'me too' or 'I was there before and this is what helped me' and even 'I didn't know you felt this way, we are all here to support you and help you better manage that intense workload'. Real human connection has the potential to solve all world problems but for now I'll stick to what I know, and that's burnout. A problem shared is indeed a problem halved. If we can reduce the outcast beliefs that we hold about ourselves when we're going through a challenging time as a professional, we have started to solve the problem.

2

What is burnout?

You might be familiar with the term workplace burnout – the feeling of extreme physical and emotional exhaustion that often affects our ability to perform at work. However, the term is used differently in different places, which can cause confusion. In fact, the terms themselves vary across sources, including burnt out, burned out, and burnout. Adding to the confusion, the term burnout appears in the *International Classification of Diseases, 11th Revision* (WHO, 2022), but it is not classified as a disease or a medical condition.

Up until 2019, burnout was referred to as a general stress syndrome. However, the World Health Organization (WHO) updated its definition and now refers to burnout as a 'syndrome conceptualized as resulting from chronic workplace stress that has not been successfully managed' (WHO, 2019). They classify it now as an 'occupational phenomenon' – something brought on by work conditions.

Specifically, remote work burnout is when employees fall into a state of emotional or mental exhaustion caused by prolonged stressful experiences when working remotely and is signalled by feeling emotionally drained and unable to meet the demands of work. While there can be many different symptoms that relate to workplace burnout, and more specifically remote working burnout, the three symptoms included in the *International Classification of Diseases* are:

- feelings of energy depletion or exhaustion;
- increased mental distance from one's job or feeling hostile towards one's career;
- reduced professional productivity.

Of course, when it comes to working remotely in a fast-paced organization, we can all experience fatigue and low energy from time to time. The difference between general fatigue and experiencing burnout is that with burnout, the exhaustion is overwhelming – individuals feel tired almost all of the time, both physically and emotionally, regardless of how many breaks and vacations they take. As noted by the ICD, burnout will often also contribute to an increase in mental distance or detachment from the job and it's common for individuals with burnout syndrome to have a lot of negative and cynical thoughts related to the workplace they are operating in.

Identifying burnout

A common indicator is individuals suddenly disliking a job they were previously passionate about – and this lower engagement itself starts to feel frustrating. It can also be harder to work; symptoms often include a lower sense of efficacy (ability to produce a desired or intended result) and reduced productivity, accomplishment or ability to cope with the demands of work.

With burnout, everything can feel overwhelming, and the effects can ripple into personal lives, especially when we work, play and live at home, and it's more common today than ever before. A 2021 Deloitte survey of over 1,000 workers found that 77 per cent of them have experienced burnout at their current job (Deloitte, 2021). Remote working burnout can take many forms, and it impacts people in different ways and at various times in their lives – just like it did for me. For some, it's a decrease in productivity, a lack of interest, a general sluggishness when it comes to workplace responsibilities. For others, it's a never-ending cycle of overwhelming and cynical thoughts. Working throughout the 2020 pandemic wasn't normal remote working; after all, many of the perks of remote work had been stripped away, including travelling, in-person team retreats and even working from coworking and shared office spaces.

When workers were forced into remote working overnight, without their usual social and personal outlets, we witnessed a drastic increase in stress levels and thus burnout. Many remote workers during this time experienced 'Zoom fatigue': feeling tense, drained or deficient in energy after a video meeting is over, or dreading a meeting before it's even started.

BURNOUT BEFORE COVID-19

Remote working burnout is not unique to the pandemic. The 2019 Buffer State of Remote Work report (Buffer, 2019) found that the biggest challenge amongst remote workers pre-pandemic was their struggle to unplug after work, followed closely by the isolation of working away from their colleagues. Remote working burnout, stress and loneliness were all challenges for even the most seasoned remote workers pre-pandemic, so it's no surprise that these challenges were heightened with the shift in remote working we have witnessed since the pandemic itself.

When we identify burnout, either within ourselves or in someone else – and particularly leaders who identify it in team members – we mustn't brush it off as 'just another bad day at work' or 'we're just too emotional'. Although we'll cover many ways organizations, leaders and individuals can reduce burnout in their work throughout this book, the most crucial step in solving this phenomenon is first to identify it and bring it to consciousness. When we move it into our awareness, we can actively investigate its root cause, reduce it, and mitigate it.

Pushing through burnout is not the best way to solve burnout but, unfortunately, this is the tendency that many people have when they first start recognizing its early tell-tale signs. Busy working environments, pressure to perform and the need to put food on the table are all very valid reasons why someone decides to accept the stress that they are facing every day.

Having worked with many companies and individuals on reducing burnout, what I know for sure is this: the more we try to push through burnout, the worse it will become. It's likely if one member of your team is experiencing burnout symptoms and heightened stress, another colleague close by isn't far behind.

Burnout is more common amongst remote workers compared to their office counterparts. The Buffer survey cited above found that remote workers are 1.27 times more likely to have difficulty disconnecting from work at the end of the day (Buffer, 2019). While working from home can offer more flexibility and autonomy, working in an office provides obvious boundaries to the working day. A commute to and from an office creates a signal in our mind and body that the workday is starting or finishing, making it easier for our brain to separate work life from home life. Office workers usually have established clear breaks throughout the working day. It can be easier to close the office door and go home for the evening, thus switching our minds and thoughts off from work.

Remote work is unique

Remote working can paint entirely different pictures. Allow me to present two very different experiences of remote working so that you can clearly see the polarity between the opportunities and risks associated with remote working.

The first picture of remote work is a beautiful opening scene. The remote worker gets up at 7 am and uses the time he reclaimed by not commuting to walk his dog and do some exercise. After that, he makes breakfast for his family before dropping the kids off at school. He then heads home to shower and gets dressed for the day before logging on to his laptop at 9 am. Having spent some time working uninterrupted, he's had a chance to finish that new project he's excited about. He then decides to read a couple of emails and check in to say hello to some of his colleagues. He takes his lunch break, which is longer than usual so he can do some grocery shopping and run some errands. He ensures he has a delicious healthy lunch and is ready for an afternoon of meetings and collaboration. After an afternoon of high-quality and focused discussions, he feels clear on his output requirements for this week and spends the afternoon working on those tasks. After his meetings, he brings the dog for another walk and soaks up the last of the sunshine for the day. He finishes his day at 5.30, feeling accomplished and confident in his plans for the rest of the working week. He shuts his laptop and turns his phone to airplane mode. He spends the evening relaxing, having dinner, and playing games with his family. He reads and goes to sleep. He knows tomorrow will be just as wonderful.

The second picture is bleaker. The opening scene sees a remote worker hitting snooze on the alarm for the 10th time this morning. Eventually, he pulls himself out of bed at 8.50 am and manages to grab a cup of coffee before opening up his laptop. He's presented with a sea of red notifications and pings as he scrolls through his 100+ emails. By noon, he's managed to get through some of the emails and messages but would have gotten much more done if he hadn't had to spend 1.5 hours in a poor-quality meeting that didn't have an agenda. He should be taking lunch, but instead he decides to make some toast and jam and work through his lunch break to get some of his work done. He eats at the laptop, working his way through emails before looking at his tasks for the week. He pulls open his project management board and starts to feel overwhelmed, wondering where to start. He decides to commit to a minor task but struggles to focus. He gets a notification that he has another team meeting in 20 minutes. Another message pops up in his team messaging channel. At this rate, he thinks he'll need to work until at least 8 pm. After the team meeting, he's no clearer on his priorities, so he decides to get 'stuck in' and try to complete as many as he can before his next meeting at 3.30 pm. He gets some work done in between and feels utterly exhausted after the team meeting, and his inbox is nearly full again. His eyes are stinging from looking at the screen of emails, notifications and tasks all day, but he decides to clear out his inbox and try to get another job done. By the time he finishes, it's 7.30 pm. He's realized he didn't eat properly today, get fresh air or even see another person but he's too exhausted to do anything tonight. He decides to order a takeaway and watch some television to wind down from the day. As he tries to sleep, he can't stop thinking about work and all the things he has to do. It doesn't help that he's been aimlessly checking his work notifications all evening. He hopes tomorrow will be better.

Although these two stories may be extreme on both ends of the scale, they can help us understand the difference between healthy and unhealthy remote working. This is not to say that healthy remote working never includes stress; the modern-day workplace and world we live in make it nearly impossible not to come up against stressors. However, by painting these two very different pictures, we can see how easy it can be for individuals to fall and stay stuck in unhealthy habits. Those unhealthy habits are not always a direct result of the individual's choices. In the second picture, it's true that the remote worker might be directly responsible for his morning and evening habits, but if he's constantly overwhelmed and unsure of his work, stuck in meetings all day and bombarded with emails, you can see how difficult it might be to find the motivation needed to live more healthily.

While this doesn't paint a full picture of everyone's situation with burnout and remote working, it helps us view the causes of burnout as a multilayered problem that requires a multilayered solution.

The stress cycle

In helping us to understand the different types of burnout, it's essential to look into the stress cycle and how it impacts our internal systems as humans. Gabor Maté (2019) proposes that the experience of stress has three components:

1 The event, physical or emotional, that the organism interprets as threatening. This is the stress stimulus, also called the stressor.

2 The processing system that experiences and interprets the meaning of the stressor. In the case of human beings, this processing system is the nervous system, in particular the brain.

3 The stress response, which consists of various physiological and behavioural adjustments made to react to the perceived stressor.

Everyone interprets life differently, through a lens of their perceptions created by their reality. Therefore, we're all going to have different 'threats' or 'triggers'. For remote workers, a trigger might be a conversation with a leader about underperformance or for others, it could be receiving a strongly worded email from a client late in the evening. Certain events and situations will trigger the stress response differently in everyone.

So what do our stressors all have in common?

Ultimately, they all represent the absence or loss of something that the organism perceives as necessary for survival. The stress trigger about underperformance triggers your need for your job to survive. The stress trigger with an aggressive colleague triggers your need for connection with other humans to survive. If an individual faces stress triggers continuously, this is what causes burnout.

Listening to our nervous systems

Understanding the symptoms of stress and anxiety in our bodies is crucial in defining and personalizing self-care. When we understand our own bodies and what states we are operating in, we're better able to reduce ongoing stress and mitigate the risk of burnout. To understand these symptoms, you'll need to understand the systems that govern them — specifically, the sympathetic and parasympathetic nervous systems.

Most people in today's professional world are operating in fight or flight mode. The fight or flight response is the physiological response that happens when we perceive a threat, harmful attack or an event that compromises our survival. The fight or flight reaction is associated with activation of the sympathetic nervous system – a helpful response for our ancient ancestors when they were busy being chased by a lion in the wild of course, but not as needed in today's world. Our nervous system response doesn't have a button that we can just turn off. This fight or flight mode can be still activated within all our systems – it's just that the threat has changed.

When the sympathetic nervous system is activated, we may experience a whole range of physical changes. These changes happen so that our system can be supported in either fighting or running away from the threat, whether that's an increase in heart rate so that we can increase blood flow and be able to move faster, or our eyes dilating so that we are better able to scan our surroundings and potential threats. There is also a psychological component to the fight or flight response. Automatic reactions include a quickening of thought and an attentional focus on salient targets such as the source of the threat and potential avenues for escape.

The psychological component of burnout

For some people I speak with, the threat of underperformance or not getting that promotion is a very real risk to their survival. Sure, it's not a life or death moment, like being eaten by that lion. It is, however, something that triggers the need for survival, to bring in money to feed themselves and keep a roof over their heads – hence the sympathetic response. In some cases, this flight or fight mode might rarely or never switch off. We can continue operating from this state; it might even become the 'norm'. For example, I spoke to a trainee recently who told me he wakes up in the middle of the night to check his emails. During the night, he might respond to certain emails and requests that come through. The most worrying part? Sometimes he even gets a response during the night, which means his team members are often doing the same.

This young man is in fight-or-flight mode; it's just that he wasn't aware of it. He's been operating in this way for so long, it's become something that he considers part of the job. This type of response is activated every time he hears a notification, receives an email or sees his boss typing a message. It's activated so much that his body naturally wakes up during the night to check in on the 'threat'. These are the threats in today's world.

Thankfully our wonderful nervous system can also operate from another mode – the parasympathetic system. The state where rest and digestion happens. The parasympathetic system lowers our blood pressure, promotes digestion and eliminates waste from our bodies. With more time resting and digesting, our brains can better learn to distinguish regular life stress from life-threatening stress.

You might find yourself in this state after a long walk in nature, during a meditation session, or even during a hug from a loved one. Our breathing is more natural and slower, our shoulders are relaxed and our jaws aren't clenched.

As you're reading this, what mode do you think your nervous system is in? Are you aware of your breath as you read this? How does your body feel? Is there tension in your shoulders, jaws or hands? Relax your tongue from the roof of your mouth and take a deep breath in through your nose. Are you able to increase the duration of your inhale? Maybe four, five, six or seven seconds? Can you bring that breath all the way down into your lower abdomen? Can you feel the breath move in through your nose, expanding into your chest and down into the depths of your lungs?

On your exhales, through your mouth, feel free to let out a sigh if you feel called to. Maybe a sigh for each problem or concern that's been niggling at you today. You are exhaling the energy of stress out of your body. You are relaxing your system by acknowledging the present moment. Taking time out of our day for these small moments can really help us come back to a place of inner peace and calm and thus bring us back into rest and digest.

How do you know if you are experiencing burnout?

Burnout often has a progressive onset – meaning it gradually emerges over time. It is crucial to remember that burnout is *not* just an individual problem. Burnout is the result of multiple factors in the work environment and is caused by stress. How we all experience and perceive stress is different. Essentially, though, we experience stress when the job demands we face – physical, emotional or otherwise – are more significant than the resources and bandwidth that we have.

To help determine if you or someone you know may be experiencing loneliness aligned with remote working burnout, ask yourself:

- Have you become cynical or critical at work?
- Do you drag yourself to work and have trouble getting started?
- Do you struggle to switch off from work completely?

- Have you become irritable or impatient with co-workers, customers or clients?
- Do you lack the energy to be consistently productive?
- Do you find it hard to concentrate?
- Do you lack satisfaction from your achievements?
- Do you feel disillusioned about your job?
- Are you using food, drugs or alcohol to feel better or simply not feel?
- Have your sleep habits changed?
- Are you troubled by unexplained headaches, stomach or bowel problems, or other physical complaints?
- Have you experienced heightened emotional reactions to work situations that typically wouldn't have bothered you before?

WHAT TO DO IF YOU'RE EXPERIENCING BURNOUT

My work and this book are primarily focused on burnout as a systemic problem within the organizations we work in. If you or a team member are currently experiencing burnout, I recommend you seek professional help immediately in the form of a registered therapist. While this book can support you in identifying the reasons for your burnout, it is in no way a way to treat burnout on an individual level and doesn't cater to the personal situations and circumstances of every person. In some cases, it's better to seek the one-on-one professional help you need.

The stages of burnout

US psychologist Herbert Freudenberger (2012) came up with a model that proposed the 12 stages of burnout. Later, these 12 stages were condensed down into five steps.

Honeymoon phase

At this phase, burnout isn't even on the radar. There are no signs of burnout and in fact energy and enthusiasm are high. Think of an excited employee starting a new job – they are eager, productive and excited to make a difference. Performance is high and at this stage you feel full of energy and optimism. In an ideal world, we'd all stay at the honeymoon phase forever, but that's not realistic. This stage comes with its risks – too much excitement can sometimes lead to a tendency to overwork, to take on too many projects or tasks. Self-care and healthy habits can fall by the wayside if this stage is not carefully monitored.

Onset of stress

At this phase, you might start to notice that stress starts to creep in slowly. Pressure starts to increase and you might start noticing that you've no time for other areas of your life outside of work. Your personal needs might not be fulfilled in exchange for trying to reduce the stress you experience in your work. Here stress can manifest as symptoms such as an inability to focus, headaches and even anxiety.

Chronic stress

A continuous cycle of stress over time will lead to chronic stress. At this phase, performance will start to decrease along with the ability to think clearly. Here is where the shame and guilt cycle can start to manifest; when there is a decrease in performance, and efforts do not seem to yield the same productive results as before, self-doubt can become crippling. Procrastination and even further overworking can take place as a way to avoid or tackle the problem. On an emotional level, it can feel difficult to regulate emotions and there might be experiences of unusual heightened reactions to situations that would have previously been easily handled.

Burnout

This stage is burnout itself. If the previous issues weren't promptly dealt with or even if they went unnoticed or undiscussed, eventually chronic burnout takes place. This stage makes it nearly impossible to achieve work demands and in some cases can lead to feelings of complete despair and disillusionment. It can feel impossible to find a way out at this stage. While emotional reactions are intensive, so too might be physical symptoms such as headaches, digestive problems and issues sleeping.

Habitual burnout

When no or unsuccessful attempts are made to solve burnout at the fourth stage, habitual burnout takes place, resulting in negative impacts on work, life and even personal relationships. Attempting to get back to normal is more challenging than it has ever been and it can be easy to just accept this as part of life moving forward. Feelings of sadness, depression and even chronic physical fatigue can be part of the habitual burnout stage.

Throughout this book, we'll explore and learn about the significant root causes of burnout within remote teams and organizations, considering both the internal and external perspectives that will support you in either managing burnout for yourself or supporting your team and colleagues through burnout cycles.

Burnout recovery

The road to recovery looks different for everyone. For some it can take several months, while for others it might be years. As burnout can take different forms and impact people in many different ways, it's important to seek professional help from practitioners who have experience in this area. Registered counsellors and therapists can be a great place to start your journey to recovery. A qualified therapist with whom you feel comfortable can support you in your healing by helping you see the common threads between your past life experiences and your current situations. Therapy is a great way for all of us to get to know ourselves better, feel into emotions that we may have been avoiding, and understand how external triggers can be an opportunity for us to grow.

Some other helpful practices to support you could include:

- Track your stress levels every day. This can support you in identifying your triggers, habits and behaviours that are and aren't helpful.

- Identify your triggers and make a note of them. This can empower you to better manage your response to external threats.

- Build a support system. Whether that's through friends, family or even work colleagues. Surrounding yourself with people who can hold space for your healing is important.

- Go back to basics. Sometimes in recovering from burnout we have to go back to the foundations of being a person by creating healthier sleep, eating and movement practices.

- Do things that you enjoy. In life it's often the simplest things that can bring us the most joy. Jumping in the waves or watching the birds. Although you might have tasks you need 'to do' every day, how can you create a 'to joy' list of moments for yourself too?

- Say no as much as you need to. Often healing means we have to take a step back in our personal lives too and that's okay. The right people in your life will understand if you need to prioritize your rest over dinner and drinks.

Identifying burnout within your team

We're currently going through a mental health crisis – isolation, stress and anxiety are at an all-time high (Darcy and Mariano, 2021). Leaders of remote teams need to identify the red flags that indicate that their team member is experiencing heightened levels of stress. Of course, when we work primarily through computer screens, there's a lot of opportunity for burnout symptoms within our teams to go unnoticed. It's crucial for leaders to be equipped in communicating effectively remotely. After all, 55 per cent of how we communicate is done through our body language (Mehrabian, 2017), so for leaders to adequately 'read' their team members' emotional and mental wellbeing at work, they need to see their team members, whether that's through a video camera or in-person connection. If leaders recognize the red flags early on in the stress and burnout stages, they're much more likely to help their team reduce stress earlier and ensure they break the stress cycle that eventually leads to burnout.

Of course, some team members might choose to 'put on a brave face' and have the tendency to sweep stress issues under the virtual carpet. That's why leaders need to understand the major red flags that indicate something isn't right and be able to tap into the most powerful skill they possess as a leader: their intuition. As Gary Klein, a renowned cognitive psychologist, writes in his book *The Power of Intuition* (2004), skilled decision-makers rely on deeply held patterns of learned experience in making quick and efficient decisions. So while we can tap into mindfulness and awareness as leaders so that we can 'sense' when something isn't right with our team, it's also important to help the logical mind by understanding the red flags that can indicate burnout within our remote employees.

Here are some of the significant red flags that I've helped leaders identify within their remote teams over the years, as well as some ideas for how you can help if you do witness any of these indicators.

Overworking

Overworking is what it says on the tin – our inability to switch off and finish work when we can or even when we should. New studies show that workers worldwide are putting in an average of 9.2 hours of unpaid overtime per week – up from 7.3 hours in 2020 (Stoller, 2021).

Overworking in remote team environments is even higher. It can be challenging to separate work from home, leading to Slack messages at midnight and emails on a Sunday if leaders don't promote healthy boundaries. When leaders see that a team member is overworking and putting in extra hours or even working off a different schedule, it's a red flag for burnout.

Overworking usually indicates that your team member could:

- have too many projects/tasks;
- be overwhelmed managing their time and tasks;
- be unable to get work done promptly;
- be struggling to separate work from home;
- be lacking confidence in themselves at work.

How you can help. To deal with overworking, leaders first need to have an open-ended conversation with their team members. Leaders need to put their assumptions aside and ask powerful questions to help their team members see that something needs to change: *'I've noticed you've been overworking this week; tell me what's going on for you right now.'* Asking open-ended questions will support you in identifying the root causes. When you, as a leader, identify the root cause early on, you can then brainstorm together ways to solve the problem.

Their body language is different on video calls

Given that 55 per cent of how we communicate is accomplished through our body language, it's even more critical in distributed teams to turn on our video cameras. If we do not see our team, we're putting our team's performance at risk by not identifying blockers that might be getting in the way of their success. As a leader, you might notice that a team member looks very different from their usual self.

Leaders should engage in non-verbal listening to help identify red flags during video meetings:

- How is the employee sitting?
- What is their posture? When they are sitting up straighter, we know they are feeling better. If they are slouched, you can see that.

- When they speak about something, how is their body language? What are their facial expressions?
- Are they fidgeting?
- What is their expression?
- Do they have bags under their eyes?

How you can help. Leaders have a powerful intuition about their team's wellbeing, and managers must act on that and address any concerns straight away. Start the conversation by stating what you've noticed and ask what's going on. This will help your team members talk through their problems and help you identify what's going on.

Heightened emotional reactions

Remote working in a pandemic has not been the same as regular remote working. During those first few months especially, the media and government were instilling more significant levels of fear and concern into the public each day through our news, which inevitably impacted and will continue to impact our work and our ability to remain calm in our lives and jobs.

Heightened emotional reactions are common for everyone, but more significant levels of these reactions can indicate more at play.

Emotional reactions can be 'triggered' at work but also can be a result of built-up emotions from a number of situations outside of work. A trigger is when we misunderstand a communication and take it personally by misinterpreting a verbal or written message or facial expression.

It's more common remotely, and I've often experienced, witnessed and coached remote workers on this. If the trigger happened in person, in an office, it wouldn't have been internalized to this extent because we've access to data that we don't remotely. Research has found that the absence of body language, subtle voice inflections, facial expressions, etc., causes delays in workers' decisions about whether to trust a new collaborator and impedes the expression of their own trustworthiness (Bos et al, 2002).

How you can help. You need to help your team and yourself navigate the psychological complexities that can happen when working remotely. You can do that by creating the space either in a team meeting or group setting to acknowledge the emotions everyone can be feeling right now. It can be helpful to share your own experiences as a leader as this builds psychological safety. An increase in trust amongst your team will result in your team feeling more comfortable about coming to you if they are not okay.

Underperformance that's not common

When your team is working out of sight, one red flag for burnout can be that a team member's work performance has drastically reduced (Lufkin, 2020).

It can show up as errors, poor communication and even missed deadlines. As a leader, you might wonder what is going on, but instead of being confused and frustrated at poor performance, leaders should ensure that they address this with their team members immediately.

How to deal with it. Start by identifying the root cause of underperformance. Leaders should create psychological safety for their team members to share honestly about their struggles instead of blaming external forces.

It can be helpful for leaders and their team members to focus on quality over quantity. Figure out what's realistic to work on right now. Reprioritize a lesser amount of work so the team member can focus on quality by clarifying the essential tasks. Set up regular one-on-one conversations to support your team member in getting back on track.

The importance of leading by example

Over the years, I've worked with hundreds of leaders of remote teams to help them prevent, reduce and mitigate burnout and stressful team environments. The starting point for most of my work is engaging first with the leaders themselves. If a leader or manager is experiencing heightened stress, which many of them do, they are not going to be able to show up effectively to support team members' wellbeing journeys.

A crucial first step for leaders is to look at their own stress levels and mental health when it comes to their professional work. For example, are they constantly overworking or experiencing heightened emotional reactions in the workplace? Are they struggling to switch off from work in a healthy way and thus feeling exhausted and depleted? Leaders are people too, and it's normal for everyone to feel these heightened stress levels from time to time. The key for leaders is being able to bring that stress to conscious awareness instead of it becoming a blind spot. When we become aware of the problem, we can work to establish the root causes and create solutions to overcome them.

Not only does stress impact the leaders on a personal level, but it also impacts their team, whether they realize it or not. Leading by example is when a leader actively lives and practices what they are preaching to their team members. Leaders can't pour from an empty cup – meaning if they are trying to support their team without supporting themselves, they risk burnout.

The importance of leadership

It's important for leaders to follow through on what they recommend to their team members. If leaders are encouraging their teams to set healthy boundaries but fail to create them themselves, they aren't modelling the behaviours they want to see in their team members. For example, when leaders send emails or messages to their team outside of standard working hours – late at night or even at weekends – they are actively dismissing their team members' boundaries and work–life preferences. Sending work outside of work without clear expectations implies that there is a requirement for a response. Team members can end up questioning themselves and feeling the need to be available for leaders' questions and always 'switched on'. If this type of working environment impacts multiple team members, that's when teams will feel a pressure to be always available for each other. The psychological safety of being able to fully switch off from work is overtaken by an unspoken pressure to be available as a way to demonstrate commitment to the team and their work.

Unconscious connection and communication result in our inability to disconnect as remote workers. If nobody considers the fundamental right to disconnect from work, nobody has the opportunity to disconnect. Our culture needs to be educated from the inside out to promote and train our workforce mindset around the benefits of taking breaks, vacations and even regular time away from work responsibilities. We need to bring people together to speak about the burnout epidemic and the risks that it poses to remote workers and what we're doing, on an organizational level, to mitigate burnout. We need to openly speak about how someone's actions, like sending an email on a Sunday, can impact a colleague's right to disconnect, and help our team learn strategies to protect others' healthy boundaries. Leaders need to lead by example and demonstrate to their team what the right to disconnect looks like in their own lives. We need to help our team balance empathy and assertiveness when communicating their boundaries and their right to say 'no' under certain circumstances.

Leaders who lead by example are actively demonstrating that they value their team's work by carrying some of the weight themselves. Of course in remote teams, it's common for different members to work different hours each day. Healthy remote teams have conversations around this way of working and set the expectations with each team member that although some work will be done outside of their standard working day, they are not expected to answer or acknowledge their colleagues who are working when they're offline. For example, if Juan works standard business hours but Tameka usually works in the evening, Juan should understand that he is not expected to answer or acknowledge Tameka's communications during his off hours.

Not everyone wants to see the problem

Unfortunately, some leaders don't want to hear about burnout. Chances are if you purchased this book, you're not one of those individuals. Recently I ran a workshop for a small team on how to lead an engaged and resilient remote team. One of the first topics I dive into in these workshops is to check in with how leaders are doing themselves in relation to stress, overwhelm and even burnout. In this particular workshop, half of the participants let me know that they were recently and currently dealing with heightened stress levels. As a result, some had to take time off from work and most were feeling hopeless. My question to the group was, 'How can we show up for our team if we're not feeling good and healthy in ourselves?'

It's nearly impossible. We can't hold the space for people to help them work through their challenges and support them in developing their potential if we are struggling so much ourselves. We might be able to get our work done and tick the boxes per se, but we don't have the means to show up as transformational leaders.

I knew in working with these particular leaders that this was one of the first times they felt they could voice their concerns and problems and it was my job to pivot and hold space for them to work through their personal struggles first. Many of them felt overwhelmed by guilt for not working at night and at the weekends, and hearing others share similar experiences immediately created a sense of reassurance and safety amongst the group.

Having finished the workshop, the participants were left with a sense of hope of being able to make relevant changes in their life and in their work. What happened next didn't surprise me because it's one of the truths I speak about throughout this book: some senior leaders didn't want to hear it. They weren't happy that I spent time helping team members work through their challenges with stress and wellbeing. They weren't comfortable with that conversation being openly discussed. They felt it didn't matter. They wanted to focus on how these leaders could generate results and that was final. You see, this is what I deem the root cause of the stress and overwhelm that these leaders (and probably their teams) were experiencing. Certain individuals refuse to admit, see, and work through these problems. Instead, they continue to brush them under the rug and focus on business. But how can we create, build and maintain a successful business if our people are at their wits' end? How can we achieve the financial results we want to create if our leaders are emotionally and mentally exhausted going to sleep every night?

We can likely achieve it if we continue to hire more people, keep pushing and continue to make inhuman decisions towards our teams and the people we rely on to get the work done, but it's not sustainable.

I remember early on in my corporate career, in seeing these important issues being ignored I asked myself, 'How can people ignore a problem when someone needs help? I'm still asking myself that question today and I sure did after this workshop. Not everyone cares deeply about other people. Not everyone leads from a heart-centred place. For me, these are tough lessons to learn and to witness in working with teams and companies across a wide range of industries. Sometimes we can try our very best and still not be able to change this. That's okay.

There is always hope

Believe me when I say there are teams of wonderful people and organizations that care deeply about the people they collaborate with every day. These people and their approach are changing how we view, experience and do our work. I've worked with CEOs who have been in the early stages of growth and had little funds left over after salaries who still continue to pay for and support their team by providing mental health resources. I've worked with the most brilliant founders whose purpose was to create a kind and healthy place to work because they themselves had experienced what it's like to burn out and not be supported. These people and these companies are out there. Maybe as an individual you've tried it all, you've set the boundaries, re-prioritized your workload and made your wellbeing practices non-negotiable. Even after all of this, you might realize that with all your effort, the problem can never be fully solved until the people at the top become open to seeing that there is really a problem. Life is too short to be unhappy in a career that's killing your soul.

Your potential, strengths and abilities are too precious to not be nurtured fully in the ways you need them to. Mostly, our mental, physical and emotional health are the biggest assets any of us have and they are invaluable. To embark on a healing journey from burn-out is a long road that takes patience, support and time. You are the gatekeeper for your wellbeing and mental health. If you've tried and tried, been pushed to your limits and still don't see anything change, it may be time to move on. No career is worth that pain.

Below are some questions that you and your team can work through to help you identify your own stress cycles. By identifying our own indicators we can become more empowered to better nip the problem in the bud before issues escalate and work further through the stress and burnout cycle.

REFLECTION QUESTIONS FOR LEADERS

- What are the indicators that inform me that I'm experiencing heightened stress at work?
- How do I identify burnout symptoms within myself?
- What can I do for myself when I experience these symptoms?
- What support can I leverage when I experience these symptoms?
- How am I leading by example in promoting wellbeing at work?
- What might I change about how I lead by example?
- How do I prevent myself from overworking?

Below are some prompts that can support you as a leader in being able to identify the red flags that might indicate heightened stress within your team members. If you have a smaller number of team members, it can be helpful to answer these questions by reflecting on each person individually. Remember, everyone shows signs of stress in different ways so it's important for you as a leader to understand the individual nuances of each of your team members.

REFLECTION QUESTIONS FOR LEADING YOUR REMOTE TEAM

- How do I identify burnout within my team members? What are the red flags that indicate my team is experiencing heightened stress?

- What are the burnout indicators that my team members struggle with the most?

- What action can I take to support team members when they are experiencing these challenges?

- How can I be more proactive in mitigating these problems ahead of time amongst my team?

References

Bos, N, Olson, J, Gergle, D, Olson, G and Wright, Z (2002) Effects of four computer-mediated communications channels on trust development, CHI '02: Proceedings of the SIGCHI Conference on Human Factors in Computing Systems, https://dl.acm.org/doi/10.1145/503376.503401 (archived at https://perma.cc/2ZLC-4SY2)

Buffer (2019) State Of Remote Work 2019, https://buffer.com/state-of-remote-work/2019 (archived at https://perma.cc/7DRG-RZZG)

Darcy, A M and Mariano, T (2021) Mental health in America: A growing crisis, *Psychiatric Times*, 6 August, www.psychiatrictimes.com/view/mental-health-america-crisis (archived at https://perma.cc/DQ7Q-ML6G)

Deloitte (2021) Workplace burnout survey: Burnout without borders, Deloitte.com, www2.deloitte.com/us/en/pages/about-deloitte/articles/burnout-survey.html (archived at https://perma.cc/SC88-EPC5)

Freudenberger, H J and North, G (2012) *Burn-out bei Frauen. Über das Gefühl des Ausgebranntseins*, M. Fischer-Taschenbuch-Verl, Frankfurt

Klein, G (2004) *The Power of Intuition: How to use your gut feelings to make better decisions at work*, Currency, Toronto

Lufkin, B (2020) How to avoid burnout amid a pandemic, BBC Worklife, 31 March, www.bbc.com/worklife/article/20200330-covid-19-how-to-learn-a-new-skill-in-coronavirus-quarantine (archived at https://perma.cc/HSJ2-H6NM)

Maté, G (2019) *When the Body Says No: The cost of hidden stress*, Vermilion, London

Mehrabian, A (2017, originally published 1972) *Nonverbal Communication*, Routledge, New York

Stoller, K (2021) Employees are working an extra day in unpaid overtime each week, *Forbes*, 28 April, www.forbes.com/sites/kristinstoller/2021/04/28/employees-are-working-an-extra-day-in-unpaid-overtime-each-week/?sh=21778b5435cc (archived at https://perma.cc/L5TF-F883)

WHO (2019) Burn-out an 'occupational phenomenon': International Classification of Diseases, World Health Organization, 28 May, www.who.int/news/item/28-05-2019-burn-out-an-occupational-phenomenon-international-classification-of-diseases (archived at https://perma.cc/M6NT-ZUPH)

WHO (2022) ICD 11: International classification of diseases, 11th Revision, World Health Organization, https://icd.who.int/browse11/l-m/en#/http://id.who.int/icd/entity/129180281 (archived at https://perma.cc/VYB9-KTRZ)

3

Self-awareness and remote working burnout

Emotional self-awareness includes recognizing and understanding one's own emotions. This consists of the ability to differentiate between subtleties in one's own emotions while understanding the cause of these emotions and their impact on one's thoughts and actions and those of others. To build self-awareness, we must strengthen our conscious connection to all three brain regions: our thoughts, emotions, and gut instincts.

Emotional intelligence (commonly referred to as EI or EQ) is one of those constructs in life which we may have difficulty defining but feel 'I know it when I see it'. It may come to mind when we notice someone ignoring our feelings or observe a less-than-mindful manager disregarding a team member's fragile emotions. We may monitor and feel it when we buy into a vision articulated by a particularly charismatic leader.

Emotional intelligence is a set of emotional and social skills that collectively establish how well we perceive and express ourselves, develop and maintain social relationships, cope with challenges, and use dynamic information in an effective and meaningful way. Daniel Goleman, in his influential book *Emotional Intelligence*, described how to help students build up EI. His study of over 500 organizations showed that more than 85 per cent of senior leaders owe their outstanding performance to EI rather than intellectual intelligence (Goleman, 1995).

Researchers have associated job performance with EI, arguing that it is not only the ability to manage one's own feelings but also the ability to understand others within the organization (Mayer et al, 2003). Unlike IQ, EI is something that you can improve. It's a skill worth developing, primarily when we work remotely.

As we adapt to remote work and even hybrid environments, EI will be difficult to cultivate, but it is more important than ever. When we work in the office, it's easier to be aware of our surroundings, and we often don't have to consciously think about body language, eye contact and social cues.

EQ and remote working

When we work remotely, our effectiveness is rooted in our ability to be conscious, observe how the people around us are reacting to us and each other, and adapt and respond accordingly. There's a difference between working remotely and being genuinely effective at remote working.

When we think of remote working, we can limit ourselves to believing someone will succeed as long as they can effectively do their jobs. However, there's a deeper level to success as a remote employee, manager and organization. To manage ourselves and each other in an online or multi-office environment, we need to have a high level of self-perception about how we see ourselves, understand ourselves and how well we identify our own emotions.

The autonomy that comes with working remotely and primarily alone means we should be tapped into ourselves as individuals to make better decisions that promote our overall wellbeing. For example, you could have two remote workers on the same team, managing the same high workload. One worker might have a higher level of self-awareness and, therefore, understand what they need to do to reduce stress and look after their mental and physical health. They take breaks, create meditation and exercise habits, and are highly aware of their limits. The second remote worker may not quite have this level of self-awareness, and instead of asking 'What do I need to feel productive and well in myself?' they continue to dive into the workloads, not understanding their own unique personal limits and needs.

The difference between these examples is self-awareness. Remote workers most often develop self-awareness through experience. In some cases, individuals learn from the stressful events or situations they've been in before. For example, if a remote worker has experienced a level of burnout in their work in the past, they are much more likely to understand themselves and their limits, and actively take appropriate action to ensure it doesn't happen again in the future. Studies emphasize the correlation between EI and job burnout (Schoeps et al, 2019) and confirm that the higher an employee's EI level, the better their job performance and the lower the EI, the higher their job burnout. It implies that employees' EI levels negatively predict job burnout. The results can provide a breakthrough point for managers and organizations to reduce employees' job burnout.

Strategies for action to build self-awareness

Clearly emotional intelligence and self-awareness are important. So how can we develop higher levels of emotional intelligence within ourselves and our teams? Try these strategies:

- **Be aware of your emotions and body.** By being aware of your feelings, you have the power to change your emotional reactions to situations. For instance, in a case of intense pressure, force yourself to smile or relax your posture and roll your shoulders. You will be surprised by the change in your emotional reaction. Sitting at a desk focusing on your work all day can be so much of a distraction that we actually forget to check in with ourselves and our emotions. How are we feeling? What emotions are arising in us throughout the day and how might they be showing up in our body? Are our jaws clenched with pressure and stress or are we frowning through our eyebrows in concentration?

- **Create your strategies.** Choose three emotions (e.g. fear, anger, elation) and write down five techniques that you can subtly use to change your emotional reaction. The more strategies you have at your disposal, the more emotionally agile you will become. It could be as simple as taking a couple of deep breaths or sitting in silence for five minutes.

- **Ask for feedback.** Solicit feedback from colleagues you trust and who know you well. These trusted associates can provide truthful information about how your emotions impact them. Rather than navigating the office with an 'emotional blindfold', this knowledge will empower you to alter your feelings, allowing you to achieve the desired effect and helping you to manage your mood more effectively.

- **Check in with yourself daily.** Before you start your day, check in with how you feel. What do you need today to feel at your very best? How can you ensure you create time for what you need? What needs to change in your workday based on what's already worked and what hasn't worked? This empowers us to address issues ahead of time before they become problems and continue to meet our own personal wellbeing and emotional needs on a daily basis.

Understanding when you work at your best

We are all unique beings with differences in how and when we work at our best. The key to successful remote working in any team and for any individual is understanding how to leverage the flexibility of remote working. When we can better understand the components that make up our own personal definition of productivity, we can start to recognize our differences instead of trying to put everyone into the same productivity box. Not only that but we increase our personal effectiveness by being more efficient and focused when we understand what works for us and are supported with the flexibility needed to make that happen. Many organizations embrace diversity in the hours they work and provide their teams with autonomy. The working world is shifting its perceptions about the standard 9 to 5, realizing that people's preferences, productivity and lifestyles cannot fit into a box that the workforce created back in the Industrial Revolution.

True diversity in our workplaces and our teams means that we understand different needs, environments and situations. Let me tell you some stories of unique humans I've had the pleasure of working with. These stories show how embracing diverse work situations has enabled them to thrive in all elements of their lives.

Consider the founder who started to embrace his late-night productivity instead of trying to force himself to get up at 7 am. Not only did he start to achieve his goals more quickly than he ever had in his life, but he was also happier. He changed his organization to be more flexible and witnessed higher engagement, creativity, and passion amongst all of his team members.

Or the woman with two kids at home and a global team to lead. Because of the Covid-19 pandemic and a lack of childcare, she couldn't commit to early morning meetings. We worked with her organization to create more flexibility in schedules, enabling her to show up as both the best mother and the best leader – guilt-free.

Maybe it's the remote worker who suffers from long-term illness and sometimes needs to nap during the day because of their medication. Flexible hours empower them to prioritize their physical and mental health and still get their work done.

These are all real stories of some of the outstanding people I've worked with personally. You see, diversity in our work means many things, so we have to look at ALL aspects of our employee experience. How might the employees' experience in your organization change if all your people had more autonomy to create their own schedules?

Of course, implementing a completely flexible schedule may not be applicable or even possible for every organization or team, but we can encourage our team members to get clear on their uniqueness and preferences during the standard working day. For example, our energy levels fluctuate throughout the day, and if we're clear on how and when, we can better structure our days to balance uninterrupted work, meetings and team communication. If you're a person that has more energy in the mornings, you might choose to focus on project work and strategic thinking then and schedule the majority of your meetings in the afternoon.

Defining wellness in your workday

Wellness is defined differently by everyone. Meditation might work wonders for one, and yoga might be better suited for another. The key is for remote workers to be clear on what activities and habits revive and rejuvenate them so that they can commit to making these practices non-negotiable before, during or even after their workdays.

One habit that greatly impacts all workers across the board is taking breaks. In his research, economics professor John Pencavel found that productivity per hour declines sharply when a person works more than 50 hours a week (Sehgal and Chopra, 2019). After 55 hours, productivity drops so much that putting in any more hours would be pointless. And those who work up to 70 hours a week are only getting the same amount of work done as those who put in the 55 hours. This statistic is usually a game-changer for the overworked employees I meet. It leads to epiphanies and 'ah-ha' moments as to why their tried-and-tested strategies of trying to 'work more hours' don't always work.

A 2011 study suggests that prolonged attention to a single task can hinder performance (Ariga and Lleras, 2011). Deactivating and reactivating your goals allows you to stay focused. The research found that, when faced with long tasks, it is best to impose brief breaks on yourself. Not only does taking breaks refresh the mind and ease stress and exhaustion arising from working for long stretches, additional research indicates that taking regular breaks can increase creativity, innovation and ideas (Andrews, 2016). In summary, brief mental breaks increase productivity and performance.

While organizations might promote taking breaks amongst their team members, it's vital that teams are set up for success and fully supported in being able to take time away from work throughout their day. For example, suggesting to a team member that they take a lunch break is a standard best practice for leaders. However, if leaders haven't checked how realistic it is for their team members to switch off for an hour, then they're missing a key element of support. It's easy to suggest that team members take a break, but it's even more important that they feel safe, secure and confident in being able to walk away from their work for a certain period of time. If their calendars are full of back-to-back meetings and they aren't sure how they can even find 30 minutes to heat up their lunch, then leaders need to probe deeper to find more realistic solutions. If team members don't feel safe to take a break (they might feel guilt or fear) leaders need to understand how they can create psychological safety amongst their team (this is covered in later sections).

The quality of breaks also has an impact on performance and team wellbeing. For example, a break that consists of moving from a work screen to a smartphone screen with endless scrolling for 20 minutes most likely isn't going to support and promote a feeling of being refreshed. Research has found that activities like social networking can significantly increase stress, rendering a social media break detrimental (Dick, 2013). On the other hand, movement such as taking walking breaks in between work has been proven to improve creativity. A study from Stanford University showed that when people tackled mental tasks that required imagination, walking led to more creative thinking than sitting did (Oppezzo and Schwartz, 2014).

Supporting our wellbeing as remote workers

So aside from taking regular high-quality breaks, what else can we do to support our own and our team's mental, emotional and physical wellbeing when working from home?

When we're physically separated from our teams and spending a good portion of our workdays on Zoom, it can be challenging to always feel at our best. By understanding the habits and practices that work best for us, we are able to support ourselves and our team in feeling more energized throughout the workday and setting ourselves up for success

There are four major areas of wellbeing to consider in maintaining your energy throughout your workday:

- creating healthy boundaries
- wind-up routine

- wind-down routine
- workday habits

Creating healthy boundaries

Boundaries are important, especially for those of us that work in a remote environment. For some of us, it can be challenging to create boundaries that help separate work from home when we are living and working in the same space.

So what is a boundary? It is a container around your time, mental and emotional energy, relationships, physical body, and energy resources. Defining and setting your boundaries provides you with a set of rules to operate by and tells others how you'd like to be treated.

It's common for people to struggle with setting boundaries in their work and lives. Oftentimes there is a limiting self-belief that prevents people from doing what they need to do for themselves and their wellbeing. For example, an employee struggling to set a boundary with switching off from work might have a scary limiting belief that if they don't respond they'll get fired or not be seen as an employee who cares about their work. These scary beliefs can often be illogical and irrational, but they can have a certain hold over us and our ability to take the next step in our wellbeing.

Organizations should consider how they are actively promoting and respecting healthy boundaries within their teams so that employees can feel safe to create the practices that they need, both in and out of the workplace. Does your team feel safe to set boundaries at work? Do you feel safe to set boundaries at work?

At work, there are three different types of boundaries:

- physical boundaries
- emotional boundaries
- mental boundaries

Physical boundaries include tangible limits regarding your personal space. Creating a designated space for work at home is a healthy physical boundary. Although it might be tempting to work from the couch or the kitchen table, having your own dedicated working space, if possible, could really make the difference in helping you to separate work and home life.

Emotional boundaries relate to your identity and your feelings. Some emotional responses can prevent you from creating healthy boundaries. For example, you might take on tasks because you feel uncomfortable saying no, or maybe you have a fear of not belonging or missing out.

Mental boundaries refer to your thoughts and personal belief system. Setting your core working hours and location is a great start to setting your mental boundaries. You can also leverage technology like 'do not disturb' mode on chat platforms when you need dedicated time to conduct focused work or you want to let people know that you can't respond immediately to their request.

Physical boundaries are much easier to see and to set, but it is important to have strong emotional and mental boundaries, too. Taking time to set and reinforce your boundaries will help you protect what you value and open the door to the experiences that will help you grow and thrive.

Here are some common boundaries that can help you and your team to get started in creating healthier work environments:

- Creating boundaries around how you start your day. Instead of logging on to check work notifications immediately when you wake up, can you create some time and space for yourself in the morning before the workday starts?

- Breaks throughout your workday. It might seem unrealistic to set a longer break during your day. A good start can be to block off a smaller chunk of time, such as 20 minutes, in your calendar. Start realistic and increase your breaks over time.

- Creating boundaries at the end of your workday. Having a regular and standard time to finish work can help with the separation of work and home when working remotely.

- Boundaries around notifications and communication.

If you or a team member find it challenging to switch off from work, it's important to understand what the 'trigger' is that causes the brain to switch back into work-related activities. For many people it's having work-related updates and notifications on their phone. This can be justified in some cases, such as when a project is critical or something needs immediate attention. However, many people are constantly connected to their work outside of their core working hours even when urgency isn't present. Considering healthier boundaries around technology, like 'do not disturb' mode, muting notifications or even deleting work-related apps from personal phones can increase the likelihood of these boundaries being fulfilled.

The mental block with boundaries

I've worked with thousands of individuals around setting boundaries and a common block is often fear. In considering setting a boundary around when the workday ends, our mind can present us with sometimes irrational thoughts like, 'My team will think I don't care about our work' or 'I'll be letting others down if I take this break and miss something important.' This fear, guilt or even shame can present itself to even the most rational individual. One way I recommend all team members to overcome these mental blocks is to create space to voice their 'inner chatter' together. If you're experiencing this fear about slowing down and taking the time to integrate and process anything that's been coming up for you lately, you have nothing to be afraid of. It is within our ability to slow down and to process the uncomfortable, so that we will be re-inspired and navigated to new energies and creations within our business. When we slow down, we must trust that in doing so, we're being led to a deeper version of our purpose and productivity.

The present moment is offering you new insight for the future of your work. Slowing down doesn't mean that your success washes away. Slowing down doesn't mean that everything you have accomplished will be lost. If you've slowed down before, it can be helpful to consider how doing so helped you in your work and life.

Creating a time where team members can reflect on their boundaries together in a safe space helps them know that they are not alone in their concerns around creating boundaries. When I get teams to share this together, everyone is usually surprised that they've all felt the same at some point. This promotes reassurance amongst the group. For example, if we are all worried that by taking a break we'll let each other down, now that we've openly discussed it we've realized it's not true and we've reassured ourselves and each other.

Consider the following to identify the boundaries you need to set to support yourself and your wellbeing while working remotely. You can also use this exercise as part of your team discussions:

- What's one healthy boundary I need to create for myself today?
- Is there a scary belief that's holding me back from setting that boundary?
- If so, is there any significant evidence to support that scary belief?
- Based on that, is my scary belief true? How might I tackle this?

Here is an example of the answers to these questions:

Question: What's one healthy boundary I need to create for myself today?

Answer: I need to commit to finishing work at 5.30 pm.

Question: Is there a scary belief that's holding me back from setting that boundary?

Answer: That I'll be seen as a poor performer and get in trouble.

Question: If so, is there any significant evidence to support that scary belief?

Answer: Not really; I've never heard of performance issues due to finishing work on time. In fact, I've witnessed some people in my organization get promoted who finish at a reasonable time.

Question: Based on that, is my scary belief true? How might I tackle this?

Answer: My scary belief isn't true. As a next step, I'm going to communicate my boundary to my manager to help me be transparent and identify if and where there might be times where I need to work extra hours.

Communicating your boundaries

Now that you know which boundaries you need to set, it is important to communicate them. To begin with, take some time to understand to whom you need to transparently communicate your new boundary so you can ensure they are aware and that you are setting yourself up for success. These may include your manager, your direct reports, or any stakeholders you work closely with. This helps us feel safe in making changes that are best for us. By communicating boundaries to the relevant stakeholders we can rest assured that our schedule is transparent and not worry that 'something might go wrong'. Another great example of this is when we set a boundary but brainstorm the exceptions outside of the boundary. For example, your boundary might be to switch off at 5.30 pm every day but once a quarter you have an urgent timeline and project you're working on. When this happens, your team are aware that you'll be checking text messages after work hours. Should anything urgent arise, they know how they can get in contact with you. Plus, it prevents you from reloading your emails all evening as a way to check in.

Here are some techniques you can use in setting those boundaries in a transparent, respectful and professional way. Set your working hours and location, then communicate that information to those team members you work frequently with:

- 'While I would love to do that with/for you, I have other priorities I have committed to already. I hope you understand.'

- 'I am so flattered that you asked but, unfortunately, I am unable to support you at this time due to <insert reason here>. Can I help you brainstorm someone who might be able to help?'

- 'Your request is important to me but please expect a delay. Today is my deep work afternoon – may I get back to you tomorrow?'

- If you receive a chat message with a question/ask and you are not able to reply immediately, let them know: 'Thanks for your message! I am currently focusing on other tasks at this time – please send me an email so I have all of the necessary info and I'll get back to you at <insert time here>!'

Wind-up routine

When working remotely it is important to take time to consider your daily routines and habits. Your routines and habits are unique to you and will help you to develop a roadmap that you can use to successfully create a great remote workday. Research has consistently shown that routines can play an important role in mental health by helping people better manage stress and anxiety (Cherry and Morin, 2020).

Having a regular routine can help you:

- lower stress levels
- form good daily habits
- take better care of your health
- feel more productive
- feel more focused

What are your morning motivators? Some people might have an hour in the morning to spend on setting themselves up for the day ahead, and others might only have five minutes. It's not about how much time you have, but rather how you can bring awareness to spend some time on yourself before you spend time with the outside world.

Carving out this time before you begin your workday will immediately improve your energy levels and help you feel grounded before diving into your emails and to-do lists.

While everyone's self-care practices can vary, here are some techniques you can use to support you in creating a more effective wind-up routine:

- Micro versus macro routines – I call this the routine when you don't have time in the morning and the routine when you have plenty of time in the morning. It can be challenging for busy people to find dedicated time for themselves every morning, especially those with kids and other household responsibilities. If you have some extra time in the morning you might decide to extend your morning walk or do a longer meditation. If you don't have time, you might decide to do some stretching and take a couple of deep breaths before logging on for your workday. Being adaptable and flexible with the ever-changing demands and pressures of work and life, and still showing up for yourself, even if it's only in a micro way, will pay off in helping you feel at your best.

· Experimenting with a morning routine is something that can be fun and can also be a great way to understand what works best for you. When experimenting with different techniques, whether it's journalling or a morning walk, it's important to document which activity had the greatest impact on your wellbeing. Over time, you should be able to understand the handful of activities that bring you the most joy and highest return on your time.

Wind-down routine

Being able to effectively switch off from work at the end of the day is a skill all remote workers need to develop and maintain. This can be challenging when we're excited about a new project, have an important deadline or some major upheaval has happened in our work or team. When we leave the office at the end of the day, it can be easier to forget about work because we're physically separating ourselves from the place in which we work. Working and living from the same location, sometimes across multiple time zones with our teams, can lead to many remote workers feeling like their days and evenings are just one big blurry workweek.

To wind down effectively, we must seek to do so on a full system level – physically, emotionally and mentally. It's common for remote workers and professionals these days to just 'stop thinking about work'. If only we had a button that we could switch on and off in the morning and evening! While we don't have a button, we can start to create practices that stimulate a calming effect in our bodies and minds. Here are some ways you can experiment to find a practice that helps you create that distinction between home and work time:

· Faking the commute – some of my clients have sworn that a simulated commute home helps signal to their mind and body that the work day is over. Whether they go for a short walk or head off in the car for a drive, when they come back in the front door, they tell themselves that they are 'home from work'.

• Writing out your ideas and thoughts – often some of the best ideas or afterthoughts on something you forgot to do earlier come after you've closed the laptop for the day. Instead of reopening the laptop and sitting back down at the desk, why not consider jotting any thoughts, ideas or action items onto a notepad. This is a way for us to help declutter the mind while not being triggered by seeing other work-related items which could lead to us doing more work.

• Experimenting with relaxation – sometimes to switch the mind off completely, there can be nothing better than a Netflix series that completely consumes you. However, sometimes there might be other practices that can better support you in filling up your cup and increasing your energy levels. Experiment with and measure what works for you. For example, do you feel better if you read a book instead of having a screen in front of you before you head to bed? Do you find that journalling out your thoughts supports you having more restful sleep? If you've had a particularly stressful day at work, what are your go-to practices to help regulate your nervous system? Have fun finding your own answers to these questions! We are all unique in what works for us and we should embrace our diversity and preferences.

In summary, reflect on the following questions to support you in creating your wind-up and wind-down routines:

• What is the one habit, practice, or activity that will become your non-negotiable each morning?

• What is the one habit, practice, or activity that will become your non-negotiable each evening after work?

What works for one of us might not work for another, so try considering what has worked for you in the past. Here are some ideas to help you get started:

Physical motivators

- simulating a commute – taking a short walk before starting work
- exercising
- stretching
- taking breaks
- dancing to your favourite music

Emotional motivators

- building and maintaining priority relationships
- journalling
- having breakfast with a family member
- asking for help
- checking in with oneself

Spiritual motivators

- meditating for 10 minutes – mindfulness
- practising five minutes of deep breathing before opening up the laptop
- enjoying a cup of coffee without technology
- practising being in the moment
- getting out into nature

Workday habits

Once we set ourselves and our energy up for success at the start of the workday, it's really important that we create and practise habits throughout the day that can support us in maintaining our energy levels. We covered the importance of creating healthy boundaries and how remote workers can maintain and assert the boundaries they put in place, but what are the habits we should practise on a daily basis when working remotely?

When we increase our own awareness around what takes energy from us and what gives us energy, we are better equipped to find ways to recharge our gas tanks and reflect on workday practices that best suit us based on our own needs. When it comes to burnout, often we realize something is wrong when it's too late – a longer amount of time off is needed and stress becomes so prominent that making small changes can seem overwhelming.

Instead, we want to remain proactive versus reactive when it comes to managing our personal wellbeing throughout the workday. Here are some daily reflection questions I'd recommend to support you and your team in making small incremental changes every day. These smaller changes will eventually lead to bigger overall positive changes in our wellbeing and work environment:

- What went well today and what was the impact of that?
- What didn't go well today and what was the impact of that?
- Based on the above two answers, what do I need to change, do differently and commit to tomorrow?

This exercise should take only a couple of minutes at the end of the workday, but it can support you in adopting changes in yourself, your needs and your workload. For example, maybe something that went well today was that you took a 30-minute break and headed outside for a walk. That impacted you very positively and you found your eyes less tired and your concentration higher in the afternoon. You decide to commit to a walk again tomorrow. Conversely, what didn't go well today was that you ended up taking back-to-back meetings all afternoon and you didn't have time to even write up notes or get a glass of water in between calls. You look at your calendar tomorrow and realize you have a similar schedule. You decide to move one low-priority meeting, which will give you a 30-minute break between calls tomorrow. This is adaptability intelligence – continuing to check in with yourself and your needs and making relevant healthy changes.

Task and calendar management

Staying on top of our calendars and effectively managing our time and energy is an important element of reducing stress in the remote work day. How you manage and prioritize your tasks can be the difference between feeling overwhelmed (and perhaps leading to procrastination) and being effective at getting your work done.

When looking at prioritizing tasks, here are a few questions to ask yourself:

- What's one thing I wish I could spend more time doing and why?
- What's one thing I wish I could spend less time doing and why?
- What does effective priority management look like to me?

The tasks that you enjoy are usually the ones that feel the most expansive, exciting and provide the most energy. On the other hand, the tasks you don't enjoy don't provide you with the same level of excitement. Understanding this can support you in prioritizing and planning your tasks around your energy levels. For example, do you have more energy naturally in the morning time? If so, are you scheduling your tasks accordingly?

Here are some other strategies that can support you in managing your tasks and prioritization of your workloads:

- **Centralize tasks.** It can be challenging to remember everything you have to do, so free up your mental load and create a trusted and effective system for storing your to-do list.
- **Confirm details and urgency.** In order for you to plan effectively, you will need specifics on timelines and priorities. If you don't know this information, it's your job to find out when a task is assigned to you.
- **Ensure your goals are SMART.** Setting SMART goals to ensure your goals are clear – Specific, Measurable, Achievable, Relevant, and Time-bound.
- **Prioritize and align.** When working in fast-paced environments, priorities may shift from time to time. How often do you review

your plans and tasks and reprioritize them? For some, it could be every morning, while others might need to reassess throughout the day. Once you are clear on your priorities, you will be better set up to gain alignment on them with your manager and/or team, if needed.

When it comes to our wellbeing, it's very similar to our working environment in that it's always changing. What worked for you in terms of self-care and wellness two months ago might look very different today. That's why it's so important for us to take time to reflect on our wellbeing strategies as much as we reflect on our to-do lists. We are in constant change and therefore need to revisit how we can show up for ourselves, regardless of what's happening in our external worlds.

References

Andrews, L W (2016) To become a better writer, be a frequent walker, *Psychology Today*, 26 March, www.psychologytoday.com/us/blog/minding-the-body/201603/become-better-writer-be-frequent-walker (archived at https://perma.cc/5Y4F-W8LA)

Ariga, A and Lleras, A (2011) Brief and rare mental 'breaks' keep you focused: Deactivation and reactivation of task goals preempt vigilance decrements, *Cognition*, 118 (3), pp 439–43, www.sciencedirect.com/science/article/abs/pii/S0010027710002994?via%3Dihub (archived at https://perma.cc/86J3-XACF)

Cherry, K and Morin, A (2020) The importance of maintaining structure and routine during stressful times, *Very Well Mind*, 26 April, www.verywellmind.com/the-importance-of-keeping-a-routine-during-stressful-times-4802638 (archived at https://perma.cc/7CU5-K6SL)

Dick, J (2013) Why do social networks increase stress? *Huffington Post*, 12 July, www.huffpost.com/entry/social-networks-and-stress_b_3534170 (archived at https://perma.cc/H53G-PLHW)

Goleman, D (1995) *Emotional Intelligence*, Bantam Books, New York

Mayer, J D, Salovey, P and Caruso, D R (2000) Models of emotional intelligence, in *Handbook of Human Intelligence*, ed. R J Sternberg, Cambridge University Press, https://psycnet.apa.org/record/2000-07612-018 (archived at https://perma.cc/K2XM-NX94)

Oppezzo, M and Schwartz, D L (2014) Give your ideas some legs: The positive effect of walking on creative thinking, *Journal of Experimental Psychology: Learning, Memory, and Cognition*, 40 (4), pp 1142–52, https://doi.org/10.1037/a0036577 (archived at https://perma.cc/3QDE-LGSD)

Schoeps, K, Tamarit, A, de la Barrera, U and Barrón, R G (2019) Effects of emotional skills training to prevent burnout syndrome in schoolteachers, *Ansiedad y Estrés*, 25 (1), pp 7–13, www.sciencedirect.com/science/article/abs/pii/S1134793718301088 (archived at https://perma.cc/9JHZ-QK7E)

Sehgal, K and Chopra, D (2019) Stanford professor: Working this many hours a week is basically pointless. Here's how to get more done–by doing less, *CNBC Make It*, 21 March, www.cnbc.com/2019/03/20/stanford-study-longer-hours-doesnt-make-you-more-productive-heres-how-to-get-more-done-by-doing-less.html (archived at https://perma.cc/W7CH-DWP4)

4

Deep and shallow work

The idea of deep and shallow work was developed by Cal Newport, who suggested that deep work is the ability to focus without distraction on a cognitively demanding task (2016). Newport defines the term 'deep work' as 'Activities performed in a state of distraction-free concentration that push your cognitive capabilities to their limits.' On the other hand, shallow work is work we do that doesn't require high concentration levels, such as answering emails and responding to messages. Shallow work is performed in a state of distraction, often with many minor focuses or tasks happening simultaneously. Deep work is where the focus is directed at one area of work without distraction.

Deep work is a skill that allows you to quickly master complicated information and produce better results in less time. However, most of us spend the majority of our time in shallow work. In an increasingly connected world, it can be challenging to be able to find time to concentrate without interruptions or distractions. Most remote teams have lost the ability to go deep, spending their days instead in a frantic blur of email and notifications, not even realizing there's a better way.

For me personally, in writing this book, I required huge chunks of time for deep work. I experimented with my writing in between doing shallow tasks like taking client calls and answering emails and notifications. It didn't work. What did work was having days or even afternoons completely shut off from the outside world, which allowed me to go deeper into my flow and creative process. Now your teams may not be writing a book but I can guarantee that they are working on creative projects and tasks. Being mostly consumed with reactive activities such as meetings and notifications is preventing teams from being able to get into that flow-like state. In the work I've done with remote teams, it's often hindering their truest creative potential.

To truly create meaningful space and time to do deep work, we need to move from a reactive to a proactive state, taking ownership over our time and our calendar. To do effective deep work, we must set and communicate healthy boundaries and educate team members as to the cost of always working in shallow states.

Within remote teams, it's not only important for deep work to happen on an individual level; deep work needs to happen on a team level. Deep work on a team level contributes to important activities such as brainstorming, problem solving, retrospectives and even strategic planning. Without this dedicated time together, the team risk being reactive and not truly able to get into creative and innovative thinking and thus execution.

Without deep work on an individual level, we're also putting creative energy at risk – as well as our team members' wellbeing and health – by not being able to have adequate time to take breaks, think or even prioritize their tasks and projects.

Remote work statuses

Figure 4.1 indicates the different remote working statuses. Which status do you lack most within your team? Which status do you need more of within your current working environment?

Focus: Dedicated time for you to work without interruptions.

Deep collaboration: Dedicated time for you and your team to work without interruptions.

Regular collaboration: The day-to-day tasks and updates you do throughout your workday, e.g. emails, project updates.

Shallow collaboration: The day-to-day tasks and updates you and your team do together throughout your workday, e.g. meetings, project discussions, messages.

Unplug: Your time to switch off from work (healthy boundary time).

FIGURE 4.1 Remote work statuses

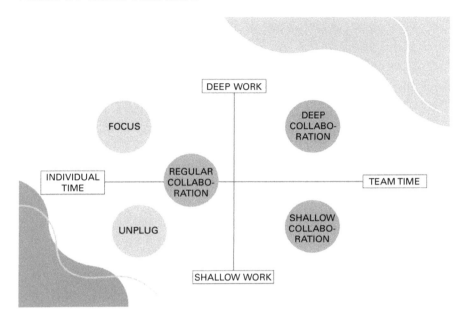

Here are some reflection questions you can ask yourself and your team to support you in creating balance across these remote working statuses:

- What status do I want to create more of for myself?
- What status do I want to create more of for our team?
- What are the benefits of doing so?
- What prevents me/our team from achieving this work status?

In presenting this image to many teams, most individuals express that they want to be more intentional about creating time for focus, deep collaboration and unplugging. Here we'll outline some of the key things that block remote teams in their ability to switch into highly effective deep working modes and the blockers that get in the way of sustainable productivity.

Overworking

Overworking is a common aspect of burnout when working remotely. During the onset of the 2020 pandemic, LinkedIn and the Mental Health Foundation found that, on average, remote workers were clocking up an extra 28 hours per month, which equates to four days (Morris, 2020). Since then, there's been a ton of research that shows how difficult it can be for remote workers to switch off from work. As we explored in Chapter 2, the reasons can vary from person to person, and from one organizational culture to another.

Overworking first starts with ourselves. Regardless of the environment we work in, there are always elements in our work environment that we can control. The first element is the things that trigger us to overwork. A famous quote often attributed to Victor E Frankl, says there is space between the stimulus and the response, and in that space, we have a choice (Viktor Frankel Institute, nd). When we can identify our triggers, we bring them into conscious awareness and thus we're better able to make a choice that serves us rather than being in a constant state of reactivity.

When identifying your overworking triggers, here are some of the most common motivations I see amongst remote workers:

- notification sounds on the laptop or phone and immediately checking to see what's come in;
- visually seeing work items in the home after stopping work, and being sucked into work mode again;
- mindlessly scrolling emails and work applications after work hours;
- a message from a colleague or leader outside of work hours;
- not being able to stop thinking about work;
- feeling guilty or unable to switch off from work;
- being put under pressure to perform, achieve and meet deadlines.

Suppose we've been overworking for some time. In that case, the neural pathways in our brain are hardwired to see a trigger and immediately act on it (choosing to open the laptop or the email), so

creating a space where we can make a choice is essentially repro-
gramming our brains and creating new neural pathways. We can
essentially self-coach ourselves towards making better choices.

IF I SAY YES TO THIS TRIGGER, WHAT AM I SAYING NO TO?

To help you consider your choices and weigh up your options in the space
between stimulus and response, you can use the powerful question
above. Let's take the example of an email, which pops up on your phone at
8 pm. You've just finished dinner and are relaxing on the couch after a
busy day. You pick up your phone at that moment, but before opening it,
you consider the question: if I say YES to this email, what am I saying no
to? You realize you'd be saying no to your partner who is sitting beside you
on the couch waiting to watch that funny movie you'd been planning to
watch all week. You'd also be saying no to yourself. After all, your head
needs a break, and you've just started to wind down after the day. If you
answer or even open that email, you're going to be thinking about all the
things you have to do tomorrow, and so you'd be saying no to winding
down. You know when you don't wind down, you struggle to sleep, so
chances are you'd probably have a poor night's sleep, too. Oh, and then
there's the morning, when you have to be up early anyway for a team
meeting.

You can see how this one question gets us thinking about the pros and
cons of reacting and not reacting to our triggers. You can follow that
answer right through until the very end, as much as you need the
clarification and evidence that you are doing the right thing by choosing to
take the option that feels better for your overall mental, physical and
emotional health.

A note on overworking

Sometimes, overworking is a result of being under-resourced in your
role. No matter how many times you self-coach your way through
this, you might find that nothing will change. In this case, it's important for you to collect the data and evidence needed to present to
your leader that shows you need additional support. Pushing back

when you need to is equally as important as taking responsibility for yourself and your own actions in your workday. In the other sections of this book, The Organization and The Leader, we address workload management and realistic workloads in depth. If you believe your workload isn't realistic outside of what is deemed as 'urgent' or a 'one-off' communicate that internally.

Technology

Of course, overworking isn't just a choice of the individual. It's not like individuals are choosing to be burnt out and overworked all the time; there's much more to it than that. First of all, while we're grateful for technology and its ability to enable remote working in the first place, we also need to consider just how technology is hindering our mental health and wellbeing. The programming behind notifications that include the big red dots and sounds like 'ping ping ping' is designed to distract us and send us into reactive mode. Our phones and laptops have become like another body part for most of us, scrolling aimlessly through emails and social media apps.

From a work perspective, we're working in a noisy, almost boisterous online environment. In addition to email and calendar apps to manage, we also have instant chat tools like Slack and Microsoft Teams. While these tools enable remote teams to collaborate and communicate in a virtual environment, it's also essential to look at the downside of tools such as these and the impacts they can have on an individual's mental health and inability to switch off. As Lucas Miller, a lecturer at the Haas School of Business at the University of California, Berkeley, states, 'instant messaging tools like Slack are particularly "scary offenders" in stopping people getting their job done because it encourages them to be constantly distracted' (Hargrave, 2020).

The challenge for many remote organizations is that they are spending the majority of their time in shallow work – endless virtual meetings, sending emails back and forth and trying to clear out inboxes and message notifications. Spending so much time in shallow work prevents us from having time and space for deep work. If a company's culture values shallow work over deep work, it essentially is not providing employees with the opportunities to expand their cognitive capabilities. After all, why did you hire your team members? Probably because of their skills, abilities, character and knowledge. If teams aren't getting access to deep work, companies aren't capitalizing on the brilliance within their teams.

Measuring productivity

For organizations, it's about striking a balance between leveraging tools for productivity and ensuring that devices aren't misused to measure productivity, which in the end defeats the purpose. Constant interruptions, notifications and disruptions not only send our nervous system into the flight or fight response, but also prevent us from being in a state of deep work.

Research from the University of California, Irvine and Humboldt University found that workers can lose up to 23 minutes on a task every time they are interrupted (Wong, 2015). So what does a balance look like for you and your remote team members?

Of course, some of you reading this might be thinking that this type of action will only get you so far, based on the kind of culture your organization has. If your company's culture completely lacks boundaries and you're constantly getting pinged out of work hours, the solution may be an entire culture shift within your organization. After all, remote working is a completely new way of working. Why wouldn't we need to shift how we think about how we work and what it means to be a successful remote team or company? Leaders today need to understand that the future of work is here now, and that success is no longer based solely on the input of our work, what hours we work or how 'active' we are in Slack channels or emails. Work today is about trust, flexibility, autonomy and exceptional remote team communication. Transformational remote work is based on output as opposed to input. The focus should always be on what we produced in our day, week, month or quarter, not about if we were at our desk at 9 am or 11 am. When enough leaders and individual contributors shift their thinking, they transform their culture.

In this way, a workplace can evolve from fear and lack of trust to autonomy and mutual responsibility.

This is not to say that providing autonomy and flexibility happens overnight within teams. It takes time and effort to truly create a productive work environment that feels emotionally healthy. After all, trust is a co-creation between the organization and its employees, and we must redefine how we build trust when we don't see our colleagues in person. Flexibility can be introduced when expectations are clearly understood and defined.

Psychological safety

To create more time for deep work, leadership teams need to develop psychological safety so that their team members can feel comfortable switching off from everyday distractions and working uninterrupted for a specific time. Psychological safety is the ability for employees to feel safe when speaking up, giving feedback or doing a particular task, like creating time for deep work. Employees are psychologically safe to create deep work when they don't feel fear, stress or anxiety about being reprimanded or addressed for not being constantly available. Teams with a higher level of psychological safety are often the teams that have established how they can build trust within their organizations and amongst their team members.

They are the organizations that have clearly defined and communicated their expectations and have shifted their culture mindset to valuing output of work instead of input.

Procrastination

Procrastination is at the other end of the spectrum from overworking and being unable to stop thinking about or doing work. Procrastination is defined as being slow or late doing something that should be done, and it's a common challenge for remote workers. Like overworking, procrastination can have several root causes that can vary according to individuals' unique experience. Causes can include lack of accountability, a reduction in motivation and even distractions at home.

With many teams transitioning back into an office environment, procrastination can also be experienced in an office setting. The office chatter and opportunities for interruptions can cause distractions which can reduce the time we have for deep work.

Some of the most common triggers causing procrastination are:

- feelings of being overwhelmed regarding work projects and tasks;
- not being empowered to understand how one's performance is measured;
- feeling heightened anxiety around life and global issues;
- being overtired and struggling to focus.

According to psychologist Linda Sapadin there are six behavioural styles of procrastination: perfectionist, dreamer, worrier, crisis-maker, defier, and overdoer (Tala, 2016).

The perfectionist is reluctant to start or finish a task because they don't want anything to be less than perfect. The dreamer, on the other hand, has so many wonderful ideas that it's challenging for them to turn them into realistic action plans. The worrier has an excessive need for security, causing them to fear risk. They fear change, causing them to avoid finishing projects so they don't have to leave the comfort of the 'known'.

The crisis-maker is addicted to the adrenaline rush of living on the edge and, instead of working in manageable chunks of time, shaving off workloads little by little, they crave the rush and race of cramming. The defier is a rebel seeking to buck the rules. By procrastinating, they are setting their own schedule, one that nobody else can predict or control. More subtle forms are called passive-aggressive. The overdoer typically says 'yes' too much and ends up not being able to manage or commit to any tasks because the workload is just too overwhelming. They have difficulty making decisions and are prime candidates for burnout.

To overcome both procrastination and overworking, and to build in more time for deep work, remote teams need to build self-awareness. To build self-awareness we must understand our unique needs and limits as individuals. We must take the time to discover our energy levels, when we work at our best and how we work. We need to delve into our internal data to understand what makes us unique and how, when we are given flexibility and autonomy, we should use it to our advantage.

REFLECTION QUESTIONS FOR LEADERS

- When reflecting on both deep and shallow work, which type of work do you lack in your workday?
- How can you create more space for this type of work and why is it important?
- What are the benefits of introducing more of that work for you and for your team?
- Where might more deep work support your team in their work? What specific projects might that be helpful for?
- How can you support your team in creating more time for deep work and collaboration together as a team?
- How can you support your team in creating more time for deep work and collaboration as individuals?

Deep and shallow work, team time and individual time are all important statuses for us to create within our work. If we work too much in shallow environments, we risk the opportunity for creation, clear strategies and deep innovation. If we work too deeply, we miss out on ongoing relevant tasks, updates and context. Remote and hybrid working provide us with the opportunity for a balance of deep and shallow work both on an individual and team level. It does, however, require us to be aware, structured with our time and efforts, and educated on the pros and cons of each working status.

References

Hargrave, S (2020) How Slack ruined work, *Wired*, 13 January, www.wired.co.uk/article/slack-ruining-work (archived at https://perma.cc/3BPX-AJTL)

Morris, N (2020) We're working an extra '28 hours per month' in lockdown, *Metro*, 5 May

Newport, C (2016) *Deep Work: Rules for focused success in a distracted world*, Piatkus, London

Tala, A (2016) Procrastination in a digital age, *Healthline*, 22 July, www.healthline.com/health-news/procrastination-digital-age (archived at https://perma.cc/QZC3-4SWP)

Viktor Frankl Institute (nd) Alleged quote, www.univie.ac.at/logotherapy/quote_stimulus.html (archived at https://perma.cc/9FRH-B5F8)

Wong, K (2015) How long it takes to get back on track after a distraction, *Lifehacker*, 29 July, https://lifehacker.com/how-long-it-takes-to-get-back-on-track-after-a-distract-1720708353 (archived at https://perma.cc/43WG-B8EF)

The Self: summary

In section one, The Self, we covered many topics such as identifying and understanding burnout within ourselves and our teams, how to build self-awareness to prevent heightened stress within ourselves, how we can define and continuously recreate wellness in our workday along with important remote working statuses such as deep and shallow work. Below is a summary of Chapters 2–4, including the key points of information so you can easily reference this for yourself and for your team.

The stages of burnout

- Honeymoon phase
- Onset of stress
- Chronic stress
- Burnout
- Habitual burnout

Reflection prompts for leaders to increase wellbeing within themselves

- What are the indicators that inform me that I'm experiencing heightened stress at work?
- How do I identify burnout symptoms within myself?
- What can I do for myself when I experience these symptoms?
- What support can I leverage when I experience these symptoms?
- How am I leading by example in promoting wellbeing at work?
- What might I change about how I lead by example?
- How do I prevent myself from overworking?

Identifying burnout within your team

- Overworking
- Body language is different
- Heightened emotional reactions

Reflection questions for leading your remote team

- How do I identify burnout within my team members? What are the red flags that indicate my team is experiencing heightened stress?
- What are the burnout indicators that my team members struggle with the most?
- What action can I take to support team members when they are experiencing these challenges?
- How can I be more proactive in mitigating these problems ahead of time amongst my team?

Building self-awareness

- Be aware of your emotions
- Create your strategies
- Ask for feedback
- Check in with yourself daily

Defining wellness in your workday reflection prompts

- Creating healthy boundaries
  - What's one healthy boundary I need to create for myself today?
  - Is there a scary belief that's holding me back from setting that boundary?

- o If so, is there any significant evidence to support that scary belief?
- o Based on that, is my scary belief true? How might I tackle this?
- Wind-up routine
  - o What is the one habit, practice, or activity that will become your non-negotiable each morning?
- Wind-down routine
  - o What is the one habit, practice, or activity that will become your non-negotiable each evening after work?
- Workday habits
  - o What went well today and what was the impact of that?
  - o What didn't go well today and what was the impact of that?
  - o Based on the above two answers, what do I need to change, do differently and commit to tomorrow?

Deep and shallow work reflection prompts

- When reflecting on both deep and shallow work, which type of work do you lack in your workday?
- How can you create more space for this type of work and why is it important?
- What are the benefits of introducing more of that work for you and for your team?
- Where might more deep work support your team in their work? What specific projects might that be helpful for?
- How can you support your team in creating more time for deep work and collaboration together as a team?
- How can you support your team in creating more time for deep work and collaboration as individuals?

PART TWO

The Organization

5

An organization's impact on burnout

This book covers the three main areas to address in order to reduce burnout within our remote organizations and teams: the self, the leader, and the organization. We know that employee burnout, especially in remote team environments, is a common challenge in today's working environment. Still, companies tend to treat individual burnout as a talent management or personal issue rather than a broader organizational challenge.

In this chapter, we'll cover the role that organizations play when it comes to the creation, reduction, prevention and resolution of burnout within the remote workforce. While the first chapters were focused on the self, and how as individuals we can reduce burnout in our working lives, this chapter uncovers how the actions of organizations have a greater impact on the reduction and prevention of burnout than any one individual can make on their own. Christina Maslach is a US social psychologist and professor emerita of psychology at the University of California, known for her research on occupational burnout. Maslach suggests that 'Categorizing burnout as a disease was an attempt by the WHO to provide definitions for what is wrong with people, instead of what is wrong with companies,' she explains (Moss, 2019). 'When we just look at the person, what that means is, "Hey, we've got to treat that person." "You can't work here because you're the problem." "We have to get rid of that person." Then, it becomes that person's problem, not the responsibility of the organization that employs them.'

In helping companies understand the extent of their influence on workplace burnout, this chapter will cover a broad range of subjects, from internal processes to purpose-driven cultures. By the end of this chapter, you'll understand exactly what responsibilities organizations have when reducing burnout, dealing with highly stressed employees and working towards solutions that create sustainable, emotionally and mentally healthy, happy work environments.

The cost of burnout on organizations

How much responsibility should organizations take when it comes to reducing and solving team burnout issues? I'm often asked the question, 'Are our team's mental health challenges our problem as an organization?' To understand this commonly asked question, let's look at the impact the burnout epidemic is having on companies globally. Often, when the cost of burnout is clear on a company level, burnout problems become something that organizations want to solve. Research has found that companies without systems to support the wellbeing of their employees have higher turnover, lower productivity, and higher healthcare costs, according to the American Psychological Association (APA, 2015).

Although the World Health Organization (WHO) is now working on guidelines to help organizations with prevention strategies, most organizations still have no idea what to do about burnout. Since it was explicitly not classified as a medical condition, the case is less about liability for employers and more about the impact on employee wellbeing and the massive associated costs.

Creating a case for addressing burnout

Addressing burnout on an organizational level requires resources and, therefore, leaders sometimes need to make a case to convince stakeholders. Possibly you're one of those leaders? Unfortunately, not all leaders want to invest the time, resources and energy into addressing burnout issues, and those that do are usually too busy dealing with team stress issues to try to convince other stakeholders of the importance of creating more long-term solutions. Not everyone is comfortable and open to having these conversations. After all, it's easier to keep mental health conversations completely separate from our professional lives and work, or is it? Keeping these conversations closed off is what is causing the rise in mental health problems everywhere. As an organization or leader, it's not that we assume responsibility to solve everyone's specific mental health challenge; many of us are not trained psychotherapists or healthcare practitioners. It is, however, our responsibility to create the space for these challenges to be heard and to do everything on an organizational level to support a healthy work environment, and provide our teams with the external contacts and support they need. It is the organization's responsibility to be open and curious as to the role they play in their team's burnout challenges.

When presenting burnout as a conversation or case internally, in my experience it's important to create the case from both a head and a heart perspective. Some leaders lead with their heart – they are naturally empathic and understand completely the impact of stress on their teams and their organizations. Empathic leaders can often literally *feel* how their team members are doing and, in stressful environments, they understand exactly what needs to be addressed first because they've listened deeply to their team members.

Other leaders tend to lead with their heads and see the problem in terms of numbers – what the cost to the company is and how much a problem is impacting the bottom line. If a problem poses enough risks to profits or financial goals, it becomes a priority. For these leaders to take stock of the issue and consider it pressing, they need hard facts and data.

That's why, when presenting the case as to why burnout issues need to be addressed on an organizational level, the true cost of burnout should be presented in ways that speak both to the heart and the head.

From a numbers perspective, workplace stress is estimated to cost the US economy more than $500 billion a year, and each year 550 million workdays are lost due to stress on the job (Seppälä and

Cameron, 2015). Another study by the APA claims that burnt-out employees are 2.6 times as likely to be actively seeking a different job, 63 per cent more likely to take a sick day, and 23 per cent more likely to visit the emergency room (APA, 2015). One study reveals that nearly 60 per cent of UK employees report burnout from work, costing their employers £26 billion in mental health and work-related stress costs (Dryden and Harries, 2017). Last year, turnover rates increased costs by an estimated £9 billion.

An article in the *Harvard Business Review* indicated that employee burnout costs an estimated $125 billion to $190 billion in healthcare spending in the United States annually, as well as 120,000 stress-attributed deaths (Garton, 2017). A Gallup report (2020) shows that employees who experience burnout at work 'very often' or 'always' are:

- 63% more likely to take a sick day;
- half as likely to discuss how to approach performance goals with their manager;
- 2.6 times as likely to be actively seeking a different job;
- 13% less confident in their performance.

On a company level, the cost of employee burnout can be significant. That's why, to get buy-in from leaders across the board in addressing this increasingly common issue, it's important to measure it. Here are some metrics that organizations can collect to better understand the impact that burnout is having on their bottom line:

- How many hours of work are missed by employees for absenteeism and stress leave.
- Time spent on coaching and supporting employees with stress or performance issues that stemmed from burnout at work (by both HR departments and all levels of management).
- Turnover rates in your organization and the costs associated with replacing departing employees.
- Project errors, misplaced timelines or unmet deadlines.

The emotional cost of burnout for organizations

From an emotional perspective, burnout can leave even the highest and best performers feeling cynical, hopeless and at their wits' end. Dealing with mental health problems, stress and burnout has nothing to do with strength of character and it's really important everyone understands that so we can reduce the stigma associated with burnout and put that energy towards finding solutions and making improvements. A great way to really get this problem prioritized internally is to hear directly from team members on their experiences and situations. Not all team members will feel comfortable in expressing their personal challenges with burnout, so creating anonymous pathways for employees to be heard can help.

Hearing directly from frontline managers who are actively speaking with and supporting their teams can be a powerful wake-up call for organizations that fail to see the extent of the burnout problem. Empathic leaders spend much of their time supporting, coaching and listening to their team's issues and worries. Burnt-out teams have more mental health challenges and many organizations expect their leaders to be able to handle the role of the psychotherapist with little to no training. In addition, many of these leaders are likely to be experiencing heightened stress themselves. Trying to support team mental health challenges, improve performance and achieve a high standard at work, all at the same time, can leave leaders experiencing compassion fatigue. Compassion fatigue is characterized by physical and emotional exhaustion and results in a decrease in the ability to empathize. It is a form of secondary traumatic stress, as the stress occurs as a result of helping or wanting to help those who are in need. It is often referred to as 'the cost of caring' for others who are in physical or emotional pain. Now more than ever, it's vital for organizations to look at the impact burnout has on their leaders and to paint the full picture of the true cost of burnout.

Unfortunately, metrics gauging the impact of burnout typically aren't available to organizations as one of their standard reporting features. To accurately get a bird's-eye view of the extent of these problems, data will need to be collected from relevant departments and manager feedback. Even though it can take some time to put these numbers together, it allows for the full truth to be exposed for what it is. Only then can leaders make the decision together to be 'all in' on reducing burnout once and for all.

The real reasons for burnout

It's unfair and morally wrong to suggest that burnout is the complete fault of the individual experiencing the situation. Recommending that an employee struggling with heightened levels of stress just 'take a few days off' or 'practise meditation' is witnessing a deep-rooted problem and shrugging it off as something that an that individual's actions can entirely solve. When did it become acceptable to experience heightened levels of emotional, mental and physical turmoil and illnesses resulting from the place we work and the working environments we are a part of every day? When did it become acceptable to witness a problem and turn a blind eye? When did it become acceptable to push a problem back to the complete fault of the individual experiencing it?

Despite how pervasive and costly burnout is, many workplaces still treat it as an individual problem rather than a systemic one. Too often, we simply accept the situation when employees abruptly quit, or their productivity falls off. Yet employee burnout is preventable, not inevitable, because burnout isn't a personal failing, it's often a sign that an employee isn't receiving adequate support.

A Gallup survey of 7,500 full-time employees (nd) found that the top five reasons for burnout are:

1 unfair treatment at work
2 unmanageable workload
3 lack of role clarity
4 lack of communication and support from their manager
5 unreasonable time pressure

These findings demonstrate that the root causes of burnout do not entirely lie with the individual. They can be averted if organizations and leadership alike start to invest their time, energy, and resources into burnout prevention strategies, starting from the top down. Developing emotional intelligence skills like self-awareness, independence and optimism can support individuals in creating healthier work–life environments, but only if their environment supports using these skills. Suppose an employee or team is experiencing burnout, and it's become a common problem within a workforce. In that case, an organization needs to stop and probe deeper into the impact that they are having and how they are contributing to the problem. Let's dive into each of these reasons from an organizational perspective.

Unfair treatment at work

Harassment and bullying at work are commonly reported problems and can have a substantial adverse impact on mental health and employee wellbeing. Unfair treatment can include many different forms of discrimination, harassment and bullying such as creating offensive comments, emails or social media posts about an employee; demoting, transferring or dismissing an employee without a fair disciplinary process; and paying women lower wages for doing the same job because of their sex.

Workplace bullying has long been a problem, and remote workers struggled prior to the Covid-19 pandemic. A 2017 study by *Harvard Business Review* found that 52 per cent of 1,153 polled remote workers felt they were being excluded from important decisions and felt harassed, mistreated and ganged up on by colleagues (Grenny and Maxfield). Just as the ways we work changed when we transitioned into the remote working environment, so too have the ways in which unfair treatment can be presented. The 2020 pandemic has seen a shift in certain cliques amongst groups within remote teams (those that had previously worked together in an office and those that never met their team members in person before). This can take the form of certain preferences and a bias against newer colleagues, with a bigger risk of employees feeling isolated and left out. Organizations need to ensure there is a fair distribution of certain information amongst all team members and that the onboarding process and beyond is inclusive to all.

'Virtual misconduct is on the rise in remote work settings,' says Joan Dunlop, a workplace investigations lead based in Calgary, Canada (Richard, nd). The reasons for this increase vary from high-stress environments remotely, to a lack of accountability on harassment best practices due to under-the-radar activity, and even job instability or pressure to perform, thus leading to competition amongst colleagues.

Dunlop reports that the most common workplace complaints being reported by remote teams are:

- offensive or hostile language;
- intimidation on messaging apps and text messages on personal phones;
- gender harassment and racial intimidation;
- exclusion from meetings and bullying over video calls;
- inappropriate comments that belittle individuals over the phone, by text message or by email.

Unfair treatment at work is a major root cause of burnout in remote employees and according to Gallup, when an employee perceives bias, favouritism, or unfair treatment by a manager or coworker, they are 2.3 times more likely to experience burnout than an employee who perceives that they are being treated fairly (Wigert and Agrawal, 2018). Remote organizations need to go above and beyond to ensure that they are creating safe working environments for their employees, across all of their digital platforms and interactions.

REDUCING UNFAIR TREATMENT AT WORK

MY STORY

I'm incredibly passionate about creating fair and equal remote work environments because, many years ago, I was on the receiving end of unfair treatment at work from a leader. Over time, as a remote worker, the mental struggle and turmoil of dealing with this issue, essentially alone, resulted in my moving on from that team, and eventually that company. I remember it like it was yesterday, trying to get a grasp on the situation and wondering what my options were as a remote employee. Being a remote worker, I truly felt like I couldn't escape from the bullying. I was constantly connected to work in my home and I couldn't escape the notifications and constant connectivity. As with a lot of unfair treatment at work, I started to doubt that what I was experiencing was 'real'. Was it all in my head? Was I imagining this? I felt I had a lack of trusting relationships with other leaders that I could approach and speak with around the unfair treatment I was experiencing. It was incredibly lonely and a very dark time for me in my career, and I can truly empathize with how others in this situation feel. I tried to change the situation by working constantly, trying to perform better, and I thought that if I kept performing to the highest standard possible, the harassment would subside and be forgotten about. Unfortunately, that wasn't the case. I remember finally having the courage to speak to another leader about the situation I was in and although I had time to speak, nothing was ever done about the situation at that time. This left me in a position of distrust for my organization and eventually it became too much to handle. I felt that I couldn't possibly fulfil my responsibilities or feel fulfilled in my work any longer.

Some could call it karma, but just before I finished up my last day I was approached by a leader who had received more complaints and issues similar to mine about this particular person. This leader gave me the gift of acknowledgement – that what I had experienced was very real and, indeed, serious. Based on what I had gone through, and the evidence I provided, I was indeed being treated unfairly by my leader. These similar situations prompted the correct action, but in my case, the damage had already been done. I had mentally and emotionally checked out as a result of unfair treatment over a long period of time. Thankfully though, it gave me the fire in my belly I needed to start my own business and commit my purpose to making workplaces better for everyone. It's a huge reason why I'm writing this book.

Today, I work with so many different organizations and have the opportunity to coach and support their teams in creating happier, more sustained and productive working environments. From working with team members on a one-on-one basis, I can see the impact that an unfair working environment can have on these human beings. Work consumes so much of our lives and so much of our time, that if we're not happy at work, it's likely we're not happy in our life. I've witnessed some of the most brilliant performers crash both mentally and emotionally due to unfair treatment. I've seen the long-lasting impact of an unfair workplace on people's mental health – an impact that, sometimes, can last long after the fact of working there. PTSD from an unfair workplace is a common result of continuous unfair treatment over time. Of course this type of treatment is unfair and morally wrong in any workplace but when it happens in a virtual environment it can only increase the feelings of self-doubt, loneliness and helplessness. In some cases, it can be even more challenging for remote workers to feel like they can 'walk' away from their work environments, with being constantly connected to work and experiencing unfair treatment, all happening in the same four walls where they live and sleep. Just like I experienced many years ago.

While I can do my part coaching and training teams and leaders and helping employees improve and survive their experiences with unfair treatment at work, this work all starts with you. Each and every one of you reading this book today can make a difference in creating a better working environment that is fair, respectful and kind. If you see something that's a red flag, follow up with it. If something doesn't feel right to you, speak up. If you've witnessed someone being treated unfairly, follow procedures. If you're experiencing unfair treatment at work, know that it's not all in your head and document what's been happening to you. Then connect with your HR department or a senior leader that you can trust. Everyone has the right to be treated fairly and feel safe at work, and putting an end to the internal corruption starts with using our voice.

WHAT ORGANIZATIONS CAN DO TO REDUCE UNFAIR TREATMENT AT WORK
So how can a remote organization control and prevent unfair treatment in the workplace so that it doesn't become a source of burnout

for employees? First, HR departments need to ensure they are implementing and reviewing anti-bullying and anti-harassment policies. It's important to help employees understand the processes and available options they have should they experience bullying or harassment. Policies can be daunting for employees who are currently experiencing heightened levels of emotions and fear. It's up to leaders and HR teams to bring policies to life and ensure that the words in a policy are as clear and transparent as possible. For example, an FAQs section can help employees who witness or are experiencing unfair treatment at work by allowing them to quickly skim through and be able to understand their support systems. For remote employees who might experience more isolation and less connection to these support systems in the workplace, it's important that they feel confident and safe to reach out should there be a problem. Continuous communication on these policies, when any new change is made to documents or even as a reminder to all employees on a regular basis, ensures that as an organization, the message you deliver is that you're taking this topic very seriously.

In order for employees to feel safe to share the harassment or issues they are experiencing, it can be helpful to define the specific behaviours that you won't tolerate as an organization, and explain the procedures that you'll go through if you need to investigate a possible case of unfair treatment. Regarding employee accountability, outline the standards that you expect of your employees, including senior staff. Employees experiencing unfair treatment need to understand where they can go if they need help and what level of confidentiality is upheld.

Of course, within any organization, it can become tempting for leaders to ignore certain standards. In fact, according to a survey carried out by YouGov on behalf of the Trades Union Congress (TUC), most bullying is carried out by superiors. In this survey, 29 per cent of respondents reported they were bullied at work. Of that 29 per cent, 72 per cent said the bullying has come from their manager (TUC, 2015). So, it's not enough for organizations to just train managers on anti-bullying policies because, in some cases, they could be the ones carrying out the harassment. Consider how an employee who is being bullied by their leader remotely might feel. Isolated?

Alone? Helpless? This is why organizations need to ensure that while every employee is under the direct supervision of a particular manager, they also have the opportunity to provide feedback and connect with managers other than their direct leader. This can create a space for leaders at all levels to ensure extra responsibility and accountability from their peers in fair management treatment.

Here are some strategies that organizations can use to reduce unfair treatment at work for remote team members:

- Have clear, up-to-date policies that are easily accessible for every employee. These policies should include procedures and processes for how your organization manages and deals with issues and what support and confidentiality is provided to employees that are going through this experience. Every incident that is reported needs to be followed through thoroughly. A survey by Employment and Social Development Canada (ESDC) on workplace harassment found that 60 per cent of survey respondents had experienced harassment in the workplace, but only 41 per cent of them stated that any attempt had been made to resolve the issue (ESDC, 2017). It needs to be extremely clear who employees can contact and reach out to should they experience or witness a situation like this. Creating a trusting environment is essential for team members to feel like they can come forward with these issues, and in growing remote team environments, it can be challenging for individuals to even understand who they can turn to.

- Assess leaders based on feedback from team members on their experiences with their direct manager. As we mentioned earlier, a lot of harassment and bullying is carried out by leaders, so organizations need to consider how leaders are performing and showing up for their teams. Leaders should be assessed not just around achieving metrics, but also around how they are actually treating their team members. This type of harassment can be easily swept under the carpet because many organizations don't create a pulse check around fairness in their leaders. Providing an opportunity for team members to voice their delight and their concerns, even if it's on an annual basis, can be the difference between bullying going unnoticed and eventually impacting a whole team, and issues being nipped in the bud.

- Educate leaders on what unfair treatment looks like in the workplace so they can better identify other leaders that aren't following fair procedures and behaviours. It's not about turning leaders against each other – in fact, it's the opposite. It's bringing leaders together to create accountability in how they show up in their teams and creating a shared mindset around the influence they have as leaders. This is about upholding a certain standard of fairness, equality and workplace safety, and if any leader witnesses a behaviour outside of those organizational standards, they know exactly what support is available to them and what their next step should be.

PROXIMITY BIAS

With many organizations shifting into hybrid models, we're seeing a separation between how employees who work in the office are treated compared to their remote counterparts. No hybrid working company wants an 'us versus them' undercurrent amongst colleagues. Proximity bias is the idea that employees with closer physical proximity to their team and company leaders will be perceived as better workers and ultimately find more success in the workplace than their remote counterparts.

In order to combat proximity bias, organizations must ensure there is fairness in the distribution of opportunity amongst those that come into the office and those that don't. This bias may cause leaders to unconsciously favour those team members that they see in person more often. It's important not only to train and educate managers on unconscious bias, but also to have managers and leaders themselves work remotely on a consistent basis. Even better, urge senior leaders and executives to work remotely full-time. This really is one of the only ways to create environments that are empathic to the needs of every employee, regardless of their location.

As an organization, especially in an HR department, to avoid proximity bias it's vital to create inclusive requirements for internal job opportunities:

- How are you using objective data to evaluate performance amongst all employees?

- When looking at criteria requirements, are you ensuring you open all internal roles to both remote and office-based employees? Do you interview a mixture of both?

- Have you created a transparent process for job, training and development opportunities for all employees? There's nothing worse than hearsay – when a remote employee hears through the grapevine that there's an open position on their team, and that their office-based colleague is in the running while the remote employee is not. Believe me, it's the quickest way to dissolve trust in your employees. So, instead, have a process that all internal managers must follow in order to submit an internal promotion.

Proximity bias can indeed be created at all levels of your organization. Here are some ways I see this bias show up on a team level:

- *Having meetings that are based around an office-centric environment.* Remote employees have to join meetings virtually while everyone else is in one room together. This puts remote employees on the back burner – the playing field isn't level and it's more difficult to speak up, give feedback and feel included.

- *Leaders working from the office all the time when managing a remote team.* Some of the best companies in this space like HubSpot and Gitlab encourage everyone to work from home at least a couple of times a month. This ensures leaders constantly have empathy towards all employees' working situations

- *The decision-making process is focused on people being together in person.* If decisions are being made only when people are together in person, that needs to change. Your remote team members will be blocked in a number of ways and you'll probably experience a ton of errors and miscommunication as a result of your remote team not being kept in the loop. Even worse, excluding remote employees will lower their engagement.

Creating fairness in a hybrid work setting can include strategies like:

- promoting a virtual/remote-first internal environment, which we'll cover in more detail later on in the chapter;

- ensuring distribution of fair promotion and career opportunities;
- sharing relevant information and changes with remote team members at the same time as in-office workers;
- seeking ways to extend office-based perks to remote team members.

Leaders that manage both remote and office-based team members should review their activities to ensure that they are connecting with team members regardless of where they are working from on a regular basis. Here are some questions that leaders can start to ask themselves:

- Have I connected with remote and office-based team members equally this week?
- How have I created a level playing field for remote and office-based team members to communicate and collaborate?
- How have I checked in with remote team members to ensure they feel included in office-based activities?

THE CHALLENGE FOR WOMEN IN THE REMOTE WORKPLACE

While gender inequality isn't a new concept in the workplace, this inequality has now translated into the home environment of remote organizations. In 2021, Leroy, Schmidt and Madjar found that women are interrupted more frequently than men, both with work-related and personal responsibilities. Further, these interruptions are associated with reduced employee performance and higher levels of emotional exhaustion. In this report, women reported more interruptions than men did prior to the pandemic, but this difference has only increased since the onset of Covid-19. The spike in family-related disruptions while working from home during the pandemic was expected, but women noted more frequent interruptions from co-workers and supervisors even while working from home. The Institute for Women's Policy Research found that, on average, US women perform 5.7 hours of unpaid household and care work per day (Hess, Ahmed and Hayes, 2021). That's 2.1 more hours than men, who average 3.6 hours per day.

When it comes to interruptions during the remote workday, it isn't just childcare and home life responsibilities that are causing women to be disrupted. The report showed that women also reported more interruptions from colleagues and supervisors than did their male co-workers. The researchers believed this is tied to many women's willingness to help other colleagues and perhaps a reluctance to set firm boundaries. Over time, this openness and willingness to help without firm healthy boundaries can leave women feeling burnt out. According to McKinsey & Company's 2021 Women in the Workplace report, 42 per cent of women said they were often burnt out in 2021, compared to 32 per cent in 2020 and it's easy to see why. Women are facing bigger career challenges than their male counterparts when working from home, due to interruptions in their home-work life.

HOW ORGANIZATIONS CAN HELP

Providing more flexibility for all team members can help, especially for women. Flexible communication processes can support women in getting their work done at times that work for them – and with these times changing frequently, providing clear outputs and success metrics can help women feel confident in knowing what's expected of them. It also makes it easier for them to plan how they get the work done in ways that suit their work–life demands.

Creating clear, measurable goals and outputs of work, rather than focusing on inputs, can help to create equal work environments for women in the remote workplace. When organizations can clearly evaluate output, they reward people for the work actually being done and not according to who is always available and seen to be 'working'.

Unmanageable workload

In sports psychology, coaches use the term 'mental quicksand' to describe how moments of poor performance can cause athletes to feel overwhelmed. This leads to further poor performance and damage to their confidence that continues to drag them down. High-performing employees can quickly shift from optimistic to hopeless as they drown in an unmanageable workload. Studies show that unmanageable workloads have increased since the pandemic shift to continuous remote working. In October 2020, the chat app Blind surveyed 3,921 remote workers and found out that around 61 per cent of professionals felt some kind of burnout as they found the workload more unmanageable than before (Ahmed, 2020). Of course, increasing pressure to perform to a certain standard, concerns about being coined a poor performer, and even termination anxiety can all prevent employees from speaking up to their leaders about unmanageable workloads. If these issues aren't addressed early on, it can lead to even further poor performance and missed deadlines, resulting in even more stress on the employee and potential performance reviews for leaders.

Our own self-awareness is equally as important when it comes to creating and sustaining manageable workloads. If we're not aware of our own limitations and capacity for tasks and projects, we might end up taking on too much and saying yes to anything that's delegated to us. Learning from our experiences helps us clarify and reflect on our limits so that we are better able to prioritize and push back when we need to.

When workloads are out of control, it's common for team members to look to their managers to be their advocates regarding what they can and cannot accomplish and to help them find the help and support they need. If leaders aren't in a position to support, coach and guide their team members back to a place of having a manageable workload, the problem persists and becomes even bigger.

THE IMPACT OF UNMANAGEABLE WORKLOADS

The most competent people can't perform when their workload is unmanageable. In my work, I see that an unmanageable workload can be handled only for a certain period of time -- a couple of weeks or maybe months in some cases. Then one day, there's a crash, a bang, and a burnout – the worker is unable to continue to the same extent, which forces change. It's an extremely common challenge for teams that are in high-growth startup modes where team members are often wearing several hats and juggling many responsibilities. From one perspective, it's part and parcel of high-growth environments, but in my experience, even startup companies need to understand that there is a limit to unmanageable workloads. The cost of not identifying this limit is usually a massive risk – if key team members become burnt out from unmanageable workloads, most companies cannot afford to have their responsibilities unfulfilled, and it might be a challenge to find other team members to whom to delegate the workload. To prevent this risk, I always advise companies and individuals to have a time limit to these high workloads. Creating this action plan allows companies to start taking smaller steps over time that can reduce the risk of burnout. For example, in a start-up environment, one of the action steps to reduce an unmanageable workload for a team member might be to hire additional resources. Hiring further resources is going to take time, so preparing the job description and understanding the responsibilities of the new hire can be the first step in creating a strategy to reduce workloads.

If everything is urgent, nothing is urgent, and leaders need to always strive to help their teams prioritize and deprioritize. With workloads, I've found that it can be just that one extra responsibility that can lead to a full system overload. Like a Jenga tower collapsing, it was that one little piece of wood that threw the whole tower off balance and led to its crash. Leaders need to be proactive in coaching their teams around workloads, not just waiting until a problem arises. It's asking questions like, 'I know the workload lately is high. How are you currently doing with managing all the priorities?' In these fast-paced environments it can really be a case of task on, task off – helping teams identify changing priorities and elevating stress from their long to-do lists so that they can remain as focused and calm as possible.

HOW ORGANIZATIONS CAN SUPPORT REALISTIC WORKLOADS

Organizations need to first understand how to implement good workload management processes for their teams and leaders to follow. Workload management is the process of efficiently distributing and managing work across a team. Recent research shows that 80 per cent of global knowledge workers report feeling overworked and close to burnout (Asana, 2020). So when workload management is successfully implemented, it increases employee performance and helps reduce confusion, overwhelm, overworking and thus burnout.

A hugely important part of preventing our teams and employees from burning out is understanding how we define productivity. For many years, and even in some cases today, many organizations and leaders have based their productivity on the input that goes into their team's work rather than the output of what they produce. If we constantly measure the work of our team on input, we're looking at metrics that don't necessarily correlate to higher productivity.

For example, tracking team members' performance by how many hours they work per day creates a blind spot around what was produced in those hours. Productivity can vary from person to person. We cannot all have the same processes, elements and practices that equal the exact amount of productivity. There isn't a one-size-fits-all approach to productivity; your team aren't all going to peak their productivity levels simultaneously or produce the same quality of work in a specific timeframe.

In redefining productivity, organizations might be worried that they'll fall short on their standards or that they're losing control of how things 'should be done'. But research repeatedly shows that remote workers are 10 times more productive than their office counterparts. A study by Stanford of 16,000 call centre workers over nine months found that working from home increases productivity by 13 per cent (Bloom et al, 2014). This increase in performance was due to more calls per minute attributed to a quieter, more convenient working environment and working more minutes per shift because of fewer breaks and sick days.

However, the main objective of this book is to help remote teams reduce stress and burnout – so we have to look at this research from both sides. On the one hand, remote workers see an increase in their productivity because they have reduced casual conversations and interruptions from the office desk chit-chat. Possibly they find it easier to focus and create more space for deep work. Maybe some of them are experiencing higher productivity because they are working specific hours that suit them in their peak performance time of the day. On the other hand, an increase in productivity may occur because remote workers don't know how to accurately measure the impact and output of their work or struggle with overworking or have been delegated too many tasks. Or maybe it's a lack of psychological safety to embody the right to disconnect?

So when we're thinking about what makes up highly productive teams, we need to think about the elements that make up a successful, healthy and productive day and how this might vary for each individual. Organizations need to ponder how they can create a high-performance team without jeopardizing health and wellbeing.

HOW LEADERS CAN SUPPORT REALISTIC WORKLOADS

Leaders need to be trained on how to create psychological safety so that their teams can approach them with workload concerns or issues. Consider a high-performing culture that promotes and only recognizes achievement and results. Now imagine that this organization has terminated employment contracts due to performance issues or maybe they've had to lay off team members as a result of scaling back operations. How easy would it be for a team member in this environment to speak up if they have a problem with an unmanageable workload? If an employee does not feel safe to speak up or does not have a trusting relationship with their manager, it's unlikely that this issue will be voiced and therefore addressed. Even when employees feel safe to express their concerns and problems, they need to have a leader that is equipped to coach and mentor them towards meaningful solutions. Leaders should be able to guide the conversation in a meaningful way that results in action being taken to address this issue as quickly as possible. Research shows that poor performance consumes up to 17 per cent of a leader's job (equivalent to roughly one day a week), so addressing poor performance upfront will not only help the employee, but will also save the leader time by not having to manage performance issues continuously (Robert Half, 2012).

Here are some other ways leaders can support in creating manageable workloads:

- **Identify each team's capacity:** It can be challenging to figure out how many ongoing projects and tasks are required when work is moving quickly in a remote team. For leaders it's important to get a clear overview of all the projects their team is responsible for, both directly and cross-collaboratively. From there, leaders can break projects down into smaller tasks, and create and set levels of urgency and priority based on timelines and scope for their team members. Helping employees understand levels of urgency can better support them in managing their day-to-day workloads and ad hoc tasks that come up.

- **Break down individual workloads:** With a complete overview, leaders can work with each individual team member to assign tasks and set timelines starting with the highest-priority tasks first. Here it's important to open communication channels with each individual to ensure not only that tasks and projects are delegated in alignment with skill level, but also that what is delegated is realistic for each team member. Leaders can ensure that communication expectations are set so that there is an updated pulse as to how tasks are progressing, rather than having to 'check up' on team members on an ongoing basis.

- **Continuously seek to discover bandwidth:** Leaders who want to create trusting and transparent relationships with their team have to be open to asking questions like, 'How is your current bandwidth for current tasks and how is your current bandwidth for taking on new tasks?' Doing so will ensure that miscommunication is reduced and team members will feel more empowered when leaders involve them in planning.

Lack of role clarity

When employees have clarity on their roles and responsibilities, they can easily see how their efforts are objective, quantifiable and transparent. In 2001, Cramton found that clear and explicit criteria are especially beneficial to guide the performance of remote employees and develop accurate expectations amongst them. When teams have clarity on what they need to do and how they need to do it, they can feel more confident in their day-to-day tasks and lean less heavily on the feedback and reassurance of their leader or peers. Having an understanding of how our work as individuals contributes to the bigger picture and overall company objectives increases motivation and a sense of accomplishment. It helps team members feel like their work matters.

THE IMPACT OF LACK OF ROLE CLARITY

I've witnessed so many of my coaching clients identify their burnout as a result of not having clarity on what was expected of them. It might seem like creating clarity around roles and responsibilities is a very basic best practice but, in fact, it supports team members mentally in understanding what's expected of them and where they should focus. If that clarity is lacking, all sorts of limiting beliefs can arise – the most common I've witnessed is guilt, which tends to lead to overworking. Let me give you an example. I worked with a senior leader within a high-performing, high-pressure organization. While this leader had spent most of her career in high-performing and fast-paced companies, lately the work was taking a toll on her mental, physical and emotional wellbeing. She looked completely exhausted. We explored where the problem was coming from. Why did she feel the need to overwork throughout the day and sometimes late into the night? What was it that made her feel guilt – that she wasn't doing enough or performing well enough to a certain standard?

It turned out that in this fast-paced environment, a lot of the focus and objectives had changed – in fact, they were changing every week, sometimes every day. With all these changes, it had become impossible for this leader (and others) to understand their role and responsibilities and what was expected of them. So instead, this leader attempted to 'do it all'. Doing it all eventually becomes impossible and leads to high stress from overworking – it just isn't sustainable. Together, we worked on creating the next steps, which allowed her to get clarity on what she was focused on each week and reassurance that her output efforts correlated to what the company objectives were. While this senior leader didn't need to be 'told what to do', she did need to be transparent with her peers about her workload and expectations. Knowing that other leaders were aware of and up to date with her priorities, she felt free in the evenings to focus on nothing more than switching off. She suggested that the rest of the leadership team do the same so that they could all create more clarity for themselves around their ever-changing responsibilities. By sharing daily and weekly updates in their team messaging channel, everyone was empowered to have more clarity of what was expected of them. They knew that, if anything needed to change, this open format would enable them to address it.

When it comes to creating more role clarity, it's not always as easy as sitting down once per year to discuss each individual's position and responsibilities. Often, in fast-paced environments like this, responsibilities are changing all the time, requiring companies to find more agile ways to support their team in creating that clarity on an ongoing basis.

CREATING CLARITY ON ROLES AND RESPONSIBILITIES

So how might a lack of role clarity be heightened in remote teams? Compared to their office counterparts, remote employees have fewer opportunities for ad hoc conversations around informal performance and general workplace feedback. A lack of clear expectations on what responsibilities a remote worker has can lead to confusion, lack of role transparency and an increase in workplace stress. In starting a new position or even getting training on new job responsibilities, it can be easier to see and identify things that your colleagues are doing and how they're fulfilling their tasks. Simple tricks and even being able to identify relevant stakeholders can be easier when you're physically sitting beside a colleague of whom you can ask questions. Take, for example, the onboarding process for new employees. In a traditional office environment, new team members would have a chance to build relationships with colleagues and learn certain expectations and nuances of their job from being in person with their teams. In a remote team environment, however, the opportunities for reality checks and clarification on day-to-day role fulfilments are decreased dramatically. This can lead to various types of confusion amongst remote teams, and leave employees with more questions than answers.

THE ONBOARDING PROCESS

One of the main areas where organizations can provide role clarity is when a new hire joins the team and begins their onboarding process. If remote organizations lack an onboarding process that is detailed and collaborative, lack of role clarity can surface.

The onboarding process is crucial when it comes to welcoming new hires into a working environment. It's essential for companies, no matter the size or industry, to always welcome new employees with open arms. But how can you tailor your onboarding process to meet the needs of your remote team?

With employees often coming from different locations, and with varying time zones, communication and relationship building can be more challenging. Given the nature of remote work, it will be harder to motivate someone who works alone in their own location. At the same time, the cultural differences may also alienate remote team members from local teams. Thus, it's important to streamline the onboarding process to make it easier for remote employees to feel that they are an integral part of the company.

Not only can the onboarding process support new employees in being clear on their job responsibilities and what's expected of them in their work, it will also help remote team members to:

- Understand the culture, vision and purpose of the organization – how was that mission created and why is that important? How do they play a role in this mission? What makes the work they'll do important? Think of it like a jigsaw puzzle – each employee you hire needs to understand where they fit in and how their piece is vital for the success of the puzzle coming together.

- Feel excited and motivated to be a part of something unique – swag, merchandise and welcome packs are never outdated. A personalized gift at your front door is a game-changer for nurturing relationships.

- Participate in onboarding your team on remote-first best practices and processes. Yes, everyone needs to be involved in this training to ensure you're creating a fair and inclusive environment.

- Connect with colleagues, get to know them and build relationships outside of relying on just office-based relationship building. A great idea could be to set up every new employee with a booking link and prompt at least five employees to book a time in their calendar to get to know them over lunch or coffee that's paid for by the company.

- Have a powerful digital experience with the company. Imagine being a new hire on day one and immediately accessing a digital experience that guides you through your first few steps in the organization. This can be especially helpful in large organizations with troves of documentation, knowledge and processes that new hires cannot be expected to navigate on their own. Take a fresh look at how your virtual resources are set up. Do they enable a newcomer to be efficient immediately?

Here are some strategies organizations can use to create a transparent onboarding process that leaves your new team members confident in themselves, their work and how their output is measured:

- Companies and leaders alike need to understand how, in the onboarding process, they can make unspoken assumptions explicit. Leaders need to reality-check and clarify certain responsibility expectations and how those expectations change over the initial induction period. It can be helpful for remote team members to see their job responsibilities in action, and a great way to do so is for new hires to shadow or 'buddy up' with a team member that they'll be working alongside. This creates relationships outside of just the manager and provides opportunities for learning, problem solving and clarification on how the team works.

- A new hire should have a clear picture of what success looks like for the first 100 days and beyond. New hires should recognize how their responsibilities fit into the overall success of the company. When an individual joins the team, team leaders should share key communications and presentations, created by the leadership of the organization, on the direction and goals of the company so the new hire can put their work into the context of the whole. The objective behind this clarity is to eliminate any confusion for new team members so they aren't left with questions like, 'Am I doing enough?' or, 'Does my manager expect more from me than what I'm currently doing?' Of course we don't want to put people in a box and limit their creative and innovative potential, but having a clear list of key metrics that either the team member or the team are measured on can support new hires in innovating around what's important to them. In fact, research shows that teams perform better when they understand what's expected of them. Perceived role clarity has been found to be an important antecedent for various employee outcomes such as job performance, efficiency, organizational commitment, organizational citizenship behaviour and job satisfaction (Hassan, 2013). On the other hand, some studies have highlighted that lack of role clarity leads to anxiety and depression, thus reducing innovation (Caplan and Jones, 1975).

- Having a clear set of responsibilities and outcomes can be critical to helping a new employee prioritize and sequence work and accomplish some quick wins that create a strong foundation and momentum for the individual's future success. Over the long term, while a role can evolve, adapt, and become more complex and ambiguous, having clarity from the start will create a foundation from which the individual can more readily adapt. On an organizational level, it's vital to have up-to-date job specifications and role expectations, especially in fast-paced changing environments.

Remote workers in particular can experience feeling 'out of the loop' of important organizational priorities or changes that they might have readily heard when working in an office environment. While organizations need to ensure they are communicating their priorities on a company level virtually and on a consistent basis to all teams, each individual needs clarity and certainty more than ever before. In providing that, we can reduce stress within our workforce and also support managers in being able to hold their team members accountable for the delivery of work.

KEEPING THE COMMUNICATION LOOP OPEN

In addition to providing a strong onboarding process, organizations should work to empower their managers to support their team members in redefining, clarifying and feeling confident in their responsibilities. Responsibilities are likely to change as organizations change priorities, undergo business transformations and bring on new projects and team members, so it's vital that employees are fully supported and nothing is ambiguous. It is ambiguity that leads to confusion, self-doubt and overworking in remote teams.

Creating systems, processes and communication channels that support responsibility and role clarity should be a priority for remote companies. Studies show that role clarity results in remote team members being capable of managing themselves, which may lead to enhanced performance and satisfaction (Wiesenfeld and Brockner, 1998). Additionally, clear evaluation criteria can help create shared expectations and perceptions of procedural fairness, and establish perceptions of equity amongst remote employees who cannot use physical behaviours to compare work outcomes.

In order to support employees and leaders alike in having clarity in their roles, organizations must create a fair and transparent process around delegating responsibilities and tasks and measuring performance. This is why equipping leaders to have meaningful and consistent one-on-one conversations with their team is so important, as covered in the leadership section.

Lack of communication and support from their manager

Busy environments lead to busy leaders. When leaders experience extra pressures or workloads, their communication with and ability to offer support to their teams can be at risk. Leaders need to be empowered to support their teams from an organizational level, ensuring that they have the time, energy and resources to have meaningful conversations and be there to support their team's needs. For example, how many of your leaders spend more time doing projects compared to supporting and managing people?

Many leaders are overwhelmed by extra responsibilities outside of their people-managing activities, resulting in the 'leadership' element often falling through the cracks. When leaders are struggling with their own time management, workloads and stress, their ability to show up effectively and communicate with their teams can suffer.

Not only do leaders need to be having regular conversations with their teams, but their communication also must be meaningful and contribute to employee and team wellbeing. Leaders need adequate training to be in a position to discuss and coach around areas like professional development, performance reviews and career development paths.

THE IMPACT OF LACK OF COMMUNICATION AND SUPPORT FROM MANAGERS

A friend of mine was leading a team during the 2020 shift to remote working and reached out to me for advice just a couple of months into his team's remote working journey. He was confused and disheartened, to say the least. Two of his most brilliant team members had just handed in their notice and were leaving his team and the company. When I asked him if he knew the reasons for their departure, he shrugged his shoulders. He hadn't yet conducted an informal exit interview or conversation but wanted to first understand what he could have done differently to prevent their decision.

I knew he was a supportive manager who cared deeply for his team and their success but I was curious as to how he had demonstrated that support since the shift to remote working. My friend had never worked remotely before, let alone managed a team of people in a virtual environment. When I asked him about how he supported his team when working remotely, he mentioned that he conducted fortnightly one-on-one conversations and team meetings each week. Then, just as quickly as he said that a lightbulb went off in his mind. He hadn't physically seen his team members. They didn't have their video cameras on during any of their meetings and it had been months since he looked them in the eye. I asked him a couple more questions that prompted him to identify what had changed in his leadership style since moving into managing his team remotely.

He quickly realized that a lot of his support and guidance for his team came from conversations over lunch or coffee – his team enjoyed informal conversations where they could highlight the challenges or blockers they needed his support with. He was also a strong reader of energy and body language and could immediately tell if something was wrong with one of his team members. All of this had been stripped away from him and his team since working remotely because he lacked the understanding of how to translate his team's culture and his own leadership strengths into a remote team setting. It took the departure of two great team members to identify this important learning opportunity.

Leaders can often conclude that they are supportive, but the support our team members need at different stages of their life and work varies. In this case, helping the team through a big transition – moving to remote work as a team and company – required a different type and level of support than this leader had ever provided before. Before my friend left our conversation he concluded, 'If I had just seen them and their body language, I could have identified that something wasn't quite right and been there to support them. They were probably unsure of what support was available to them.' Take time to ask the question, 'What can I do to support you right now with this change?' or 'What's the most important thing I can support you with right now that will help you feel better in your work or in yourself?' This gets team members talking about issues that might otherwise get lost in the shuffle.

For leaders, it's essential to be involved in the day-to-day lives of their team members and be able to identify potential issues ahead of time. In a remote environment, issues and problems can easily go unnoticed. With regular discussion of and participation in employees' roles, managers are better suited to resolve problems when they arise. In turn, employees will be more likely to seek the advice of managers, who can then offer tips and suggestions to employees to prevent problems before they occur.

Here are strategies that organizations can use to help their leaders to better support their team members:

- Limit the number of direct reports each leader has. Research shows that when a leader has more than seven direct reports, their ability to support each team member reduces dramatically (Schleckser, 2019).

- Reduce workloads for leaders by understanding that the majority of their workload and responsibilities should be taken up with supporting and coaching team members to their greatest potential.

- Develop team leaders' skills around emotional intelligence, active listening and coaching. Research shows that leaders who demonstrate higher levels of active listening, coaching and emotional intelligence have teams with higher levels of satisfaction and engagement. Supportive communication through active-empathetic listening may improve mutual understanding and reduce individuals' and work teams' uncertainty and help them feel as though they have control over their work (Mattson and Hall, 2011).

Unreasonable time pressure

Unreasonable deadlines and pressure can create a snowball effect – when employees miss one overly aggressive deadline, they fall behind on the next thing they are scheduled to do. This can lead to major blockers in employees' abilities to catch up when environments feel continually chaotic and projects are always time sensitive. If everything is urgent, then nothing is urgent. Organizations must acknowledge the need for realistic timelines and open up conversations with their workforce as to what is and what isn't possible. While it's important to set ambitious goals to ensure company growth and achieve metrics, companies should reflect on how their expectations are impacting the wellbeing of their workforce and if their expectations on timelines are increasing or hindering performance in the long term. Maslach (2000) suggests that corporations today are 'cashing in their intrinsic worth. Instead of providing the foundations for long-term growth, they are cashing in their assets for short-term stock performance.'

Taking responsibility as an organization

For organizations to take a step back and look at what they can improve on a company level, they must have an open mindset. After all, it's not easy for a company to admit that they have been part of the problem. Possibly they've pushed too hard on a constant need for achievement and results, or maybe they've introduced new employee benefits and thought that it would suffice to reduce workplace burnout. As Maslach (2000) states:

> We should be trying to identify and analyze the critical components of 'bad' situations in which many good people function. Imagine investigating the personality of cucumbers to discover why they had turned into sour pickles without analyzing the vinegar barrels in which they had been submerged.

For a company to look at these root causes of burnout, its leaders have to turn inward and understand their culture's damaging impact on employees' wellbeing. It's not about blaming or shaming any one or two individuals; it's about taking responsibility as a whole and understanding that to make positive long-lasting changes, we need to be willing to get uncomfortable as we explore what's not working, where the friction started and where it's multiplied.

References

Ahmed, A (2020) Research suggests that remote working is aggravating secondary stressors which are causing people to feel burned out more than ever before, *Digital Information World*, 21 October, www.digitalinformationworld.com/2020/10/research-suggests-that-remote-working.html (archived at https://perma.cc/XN3R-S264)

APA (2015) Stress in America: Paying with our health, www.apa.org/news/press/releases/stress/2014/stress-report.pdf (archived at https://perma.cc/28YF-7F7G)

Asana (2021) Anatomy of work index 2021: Overcoming disruption in a distributed world, https://blog.asana.com/2021/01/anz-anatomy-of-work-infographic/ (archived at https://perma.cc/67Q2-KZHF)

Bloom, N, Liang, J, Roberts, J and Ying, Z J (2014) Does working from home work? Evidence from a Chinese experiment, *The Quarterly Journal of Economics*, 130 (1), pp 165–218, https://doi.org/10.1093/qje/qju032 (archived at https://perma.cc/XV68-62H3)

Caplan, R D and Jones, K W (1975) Effects of work load, role ambiguity, and Type A personality on anxiety, depression, and heart rate, *Journal of Applied Psychology*, 6, https://psycnet.apa.org/buy/1976-05806-001 (archived at https://perma.cc/RD8B-5FDY)

Cramton, C D (2001) The mutual knowledge problem and its consequences for dispersed collaboration, *Organization Science*, 12 (3), pp 346–71, https://psycnet.apa.org/record/2001-11113-005 (archived at https://perma.cc/NX7V-3GNR)

Dryden, R and Harries, I (2017) Mental health: The costs to employees and businesses, *Safety & Health Practitioner*, 9 February, www.shponline.co.uk/mental-health/mental-health-the-costs-to-employees-and-businesses (archived at https://perma.cc/X794-HTGL)

ESDC (2017) Harassment and sexual violence in the workplace – Public consultation: What we heard, www.canada.ca/content/dam/canada/employment-social-development/services/health-safety/reports/workplace-harassment-sexual-violence-EN.pdf (archived at https://perma.cc/KE9F-KWT9)

Gallup (nd) How to prevent employee burnout, www.gallup.com/workplace/313160/preventing-and-dealing-with-employee-burnout.aspx# (archived at https://perma.cc/N7DE-B9S7)

Gallup (2020) Gallup's Perspective on employee burnout: Causes and cures, www.gallup.com/workplace/282659/employee-burnout-perspective-paper.aspx (archived at https://perma.cc/MZ98-T23W)

Garton, E (2017) Employee burnout is a problem with the company, not the person, *Harvard Business Review*, 6 April, https://hbr.org/2017/04/employee-burnout-is-a-problem-with-the-company-not-the-person (archived at https://perma.cc/2JFY-XXDV)

Grenny, J and Maxfield, D (2017) A study of 1,100 employees found that remote workers feel shunned and left out, *Harvard Business Review*, 2 November, https://hbr.org/2017/11/a-study-of-1100-employees-found-that-remote-workers-feel-shunned-and-left-out (archived at https://perma.cc/TJC9-22ER)

Hassan, S (2013) The importance of role clarification in workgroups: Effects on perceived role clarity, work satisfaction, and turnover rates, *Public Administration Review*, 73 (5), pp 716–25, https://psycnet.apa.org/record/2013-33170-011 (archived at https://perma.cc/4HES-CG2Y)

Hess, C, Ahmed, T and Hayes, J (2021) Providing unpaid household and care work in the United States: Uncovering inequality, Institute for Women's Policy Research, https://iwpr.org/wp-content/uploads/2020/01/IWPR-Providing-Unpaid-Household-and-Care-Work-in-the-United-States-Uncovering-Inequality.pdf (archived at https://perma.cc/GC4V-C4MY)

Leroy, S, Schmidt, A M and Madjar, N (2021) Working from home during COVID-19: A study of the interruption landscape, *Journal of Applied Psychology*, 106 (10), pp 1448–65, https://psycnet.apa.org/record/2022-08530-002 (archived at https://perma.cc/SL7K-G2EB)

Maslach, C (2000) *The Truth About Burnout: How organizations cause personal stress and what to do about it*, Jossey-Bass, Hoboken, NJ

Mattson, M and Hall, J G (2011) *Health as Communication Nexus: A service learning approach*, Kendall Hunt Publishing, Dubuque, IA

McKinsey & Company (2021) Women in the workplace, https://wiw-report.s3.amazonaws.com/Women_in_the_Workplace_2021.pdf (archived at https://perma.cc/8BXV-P8UT)

Moss, J (2019) Burnout is about your workplace, not your people, *Harvard Business Review*, 11 December, https://hbr.org/2019/12/burnout-is-about-your-workplace-not-your-people (archived at https://perma.cc/PLA3-89PN)

Richard, J (nd) Workplace bullying has gone remote, *Monster.com*, www.monster.ca/career-advice/article/workplace-bullying (archived at https://perma.cc/RR22-5EMP)

Robert Half (2012) Survey: Managers spend nearly one day a week managing poor performers, https://rh-us.mediaroom.com/2012-11-08-Survey-Managers-Spend-Nearly-One-Day-a-Week-Managing-Poor-Performers (archived at https://perma.cc/KN59-P7NK)

Schleckser, J (2019) How many direct reports should you have? *Inc.com*, 5 March, www.inc.com/jim-schleckser/how-many-direct-reports-should-you-have.html (archived at https://perma.cc/8NKB-575P)

Seppälä, E and Cameron, K (2015) Proof that positive work cultures are more productive, *Harvard Business Review*, 1 December, https://hbr.org/2015/12/proof-that-positive-work-cultures-are-more-productive (archived at https://perma.cc/9CFL-9FWW)

TUC (2015) Nearly a third of people are bulled at work, says TUC, 16 November, www.tuc.org.uk/news/nearly-third-people-are-bullied-work-says-tuc (archived at https://perma.cc/9LJQ-7E9Y)

Wiesenfeld, B M and Brockner, J (1998) Toward a psychology of contingent work, in *Debating Rationality: Nonrational aspects of organizational decision making*, ed. J J Halpern and R C Stern, Cornell University Press, Ithaca, NY

Wigert, B and Agrawal, S (2018) Employee burnout, part 1: The 5 main causes, *Gallup.com*, 12 July, www.gallup.com/workplace/237059/employee-burnout-part-main-causes.aspx (archived at https://perma.cc/EM6D-CC47)

6

Employee retention

With the Covid-19 pandemic of 2020 and restrictions aside, remote working offers many benefits and opportunities that otherwise wouldn't be available if an employee is required to return to an office. In a survey by job listings site Flexjobs, an astonishing 65 per cent of pandemic remote workers said they wanted to keep working from home, and 58 per cent even said they would look for a new job if they had to return to the office (Pelta, 2021). Meanwhile, the epidemic of workplace stress is also on the rise. Stanford researchers found that in the United States, workplace stress leads to spending of nearly $190 billion – roughly 8 per cent of national healthcare outlays – and almost 120,000 deaths each year (Lynch, 2015). Worldwide, 615 million people suffer from depression and anxiety and, according to a recent study by the World Health Organization (WHO), this costs the global workforce an estimated $1 trillion in lost productivity each year (WHO, nd). Of course, the actual cost to business is far greater than just the cost of lost productivity in sick days, stress levels, and employees' inability to work. Employee burnout and stress issues result in high turnover and the loss of great talent.

Workers worldwide are moving on from their current jobs in search of a better employee experience. Since many of the world's organizations are working remotely, workers have an endless pool of companies to work with, and employers have a global pool of applications to choose from. While the workforce is more empowered than ever before, this leaves companies at risk of losing their best employees. The percentage of employees expected to change jobs ranges depending on the source, with the period being coined The Great Resignation.

The 2022 Microsoft Work Trend Index found that 40 per cent of people wanted to change jobs. A survey of workers in the UK and Ireland put the number at 38 per cent (Moneypenny, 2022), and a similar US survey found that 26 per cent of workers are planning to leave their current job (Prudential, 2021). Since the 2020 pandemic, remote working has opened many individuals up to a new way of life – no commuting, the opportunity to spend more time with those who truly matter, and the flexibility to work from their preferred location.

What are employees really looking for?

For the workforce that wants to continue working remotely and craves more sustainable and happier workplaces, options for moving careers have opened up tenfold. These candidates are no longer tied to applying for positions in their local town or city – they can apply for jobs all over the world. But this time, they'll be extra cautious. Sure, salary, benefits and working hours are essential factors in choosing a new employer. However, these job seekers will be investigating how their potential new organization looks after its employees and its remote company culture to create sustainable remote teams. They've worked remotely in a not-so-great culture. They now want an incredible culture that goes above and beyond to ensure team members feel looked after and are fully supported in their mental, physical and emotional wellbeing. Research shows that 50 per cent of candidates say they wouldn't work for a company with a bad reputation, even for a pay increase (HR Daily Advisor, 2019).

An analysis of recruitment in businesses has shown that employees are more attracted to departments with a good team and leadership working spirit, which produces positive productivity (Richards, nd). Other research finds that employees who are satisfied with their work environments are 16 per cent more productive, 18 per cent more likely to stay, and 30 per cent more attracted to their company than competitors (Aggarwal and Rozwell, 2018). Two-thirds of survey respondents in the same study said that a workplace focused on their health and wellbeing would make them more likely to accept a new job or keep the job they have. This means that companies willing to adapt to an employee-centric view of workplace wellness will not only increase their productivity, they will also improve their ability to attract and retain talent.

As Peter Drucker is attributed to have said, 'your culture will eat any strategy for breakfast'. Today's talent pool of potential candidates isn't just researching and looking at an organization's career page to determine its company values, perks, and benefits; they're researching the reasons why previous employees decided to leave and what the current team members have to say about working there. Use of employee review boards like Glassdoor is at an all-time high. According to Glassdoor (2020), 86 per cent of passive candidates evaluate a brand before applying for a job, which means companies need to actively practise what they preach. It's not enough now to say your organization has a great 'work–life balance culture' – your future employees are reaching out to team members that no longer work there and asking, 'why not?' Organizations are now forced to be honest about their working environments because they can no longer just pretend. Once executives confront the problem at an organizational level, they can use organizational measures to address it.

In a candidate-driven market, having a good reputation as an employer has become key to attracting great new employees. Encouraging work–life balance can work to your advantage as a business to keep employees engaged, helping you to retain your staff and saving you time and money usually involved with replacing an employee.

The market has become increasingly competitive, with a global portfolio of companies hiring remotely; it's laborious to secure great talent. In a study by Cielo Talent where they surveyed over 140 HR and senior talent acquisition leaders, they found that the success of remote working has opened previously unavailable talent pools to talent acquisition teams, with 64 per cent of hiring managers now more willing to consider remote workers (Cielo, nd). However, it also leads to certain challenges. For example, 21 per cent of leaders are worried that drop-off rates will increase at the earlier stages of hiring, while 62 per cent believe companies will need to work harder to stand out from the competition. Companies are competitive and fighting for access to the very best talent – and the one way to increase your chances of being attractive in a global remote talent pool is to constantly seek to improve your remote employee experience.

Today workers are increasingly looking to learn personal development and self-management skills, which means without an explicit learning and development strategy for your employees, you're not only putting your organization's growth at risk, you'll also risk losing your best talent. If the Covid-19 pandemic has taught us anything in the remote environment, it's this:

> The success of remote employees is not based on their ability to do their jobs and fulfil their duties. It's based on their ability to self-manage and regulate themselves through self-awareness and their organization's and leaders' ability to create a remote employee experience that reduces friction and stress.

Executives need to own up to their role in creating the workplace stress that leads to burnout – heavy workloads, job insecurity, and frustrating work routines that include too many meetings and far too little time for creative work.

Early intervention offers the possibility to mitigate damage. While it takes an average of 14 months to two years to recover from full-blown burnout, catching burnout upstream in an earlier phase can reduce the cost and length of interventions. To do this requires organizational awareness from leadership and managers, as well as regular collection of burnout-related data at the individual, team, and aggregate levels. It also requires companies to better understand the skills and abilities that are needed in order to be successful at remote working. When organizations understand this, they can create a more optimized hiring process for remote team environments.

The importance of hiring for remote

Organizations need to consider assessing candidates for the abilities and skill sets that support them to work effectively remotely, especially as the transition to hybrid working becomes even more popular amongst organizations. Remote working is not for everyone, and it takes a particular skill set and abilities to work independently at home. There are many traits and skills that organizations can assess during the hiring process to identify if candidates are suited for a work-from-home position. While many of today's workforce now have some level of experience in virtual working, it can be helpful to build remote working assessments into the interview process.

Aside from the skills and traits required for the specific position itself, there are some general attributes a solid remote worker has. You may state that 'remote working is required' on your job spec; however, it's important to take the time to evaluate each candidate's experience of remote working, and how they've navigated the complexities and challenges that remote working can often bring, such as isolation, miscommunication and even managing their own wellbeing while working from home. To help us understand these skills, emotional intelligence could be the answer.

Similarly, in a hybrid environment, workers need to be able to understand themselves, their energy levels and their personality types so that they can better manage their energy between being in person and working at home alone. It's vital for successful hybrid teams to understand how to use the locations of home working and office working to their advantage by understanding which elements of work are better suited to each environment. For example, deep collaboration as a team is better scheduled in the office in person, while deep work alone is better for home working.

The emotional intelligence of hiring

Emotional intelligence is a set of emotional and social skills that collectively establish how well we perceive and express ourselves, develop and maintain social relationships, cope with challenges, and use emotional information in an effective and meaningful way.

When we think of remote working, we shouldn't limit ourselves to believing someone will succeed as long as they can effectively do their jobs. There are deeper-level skills to being successful as a remote employee, manager and organization. In order to manage ourselves and each other in an online or multi-office environment, individuals need to have a high level of self-perception – how we see ourselves, understand ourselves and how well we identify our own emotions.

The autonomy that comes with working remotely, and primarily alone, means we should tap into ourselves as individuals in order to better make decisions that promote our overall wellbeing. Often remote team members need high levels of independence, and working without in-person interactions on a daily basis means we need to adjust how we express ourselves online.

Our communication skills and awareness should be developed when we're working in multicultural virtual environments. We need to understand how we can communicate, listen and express ourselves effectively online. If our teammates are based all over the world, we need to develop our independence in order to be resourceful and self-sufficient.

Our assertiveness in setting clear and healthy boundaries and expectations is vital when working across multiple time zones and primarily online when we're so connected through technology. Our interpersonal skills need to be developed and explored when we work online with colleagues, employees and customers. In order to build mutually satisfying, trusting relationships, we need to develop our empathy towards other people

Given all this, it can be helpful to understand the exact expectations of each candidate and build a customized interview question process around their potential future working situation. For example, if you require a candidate to work across multiple time zones, it can be helpful to assess the skills that either supported them in doing this in a previous job or what skills they think they would need to effectively manage communication across time zones.

Here are some questions organizations can reflect upon to help them consider more of the details for each candidate's remote working environment:

- Do you want the candidate to be in specific time zones?
- Do you have a specific expectation of how much time should be spent online?
- How will your processes be documented and organized?
- How much of the role is expected to be independent and what 'top-down' processes and procedures are to be maintained?

Table 6.1 gives some example questions based on the emotional intelligence skills mentioned above that can support your organization in assessing remote working skills during the interview process.

TABLE 6.1 Hiring questions for remote working EQ skills

EQ (emotional intelligence) skill	Ways to assess
Self-awareness	When do they work at their best? How best do they problem-solve/make decisions/be productive? What are their strengths and weaknesses?
Interpersonal relationships	How have they built a relationship with you and the team throughout the interview processes? Do they have the ability to build mutually beneficial relationships with colleagues, customers and partners online?
Flexibility	How have they adapted in the past to team/business changes? How do they adapt themselves when they go through change? How will they ensure they are set up for success in this new role?
Empathy	How has the candidate communicated over written text and video calls? With working in any remote and multi-location environment, their communication skills will need to be top-notch. Are they able to express themselves, their ideas and experiences clearly while also considering others' points of view?
Assertiveness	Can they articulate and express their beliefs and ideas in a non-offensive but clear way?
Optimism	How have they remained positive in the face of adversity?
Independence	How well do they work alone? How have they demonstrated resourcefulness in the past?

The hustle culture

Often, it's not about what organizations do but how they do it. Companies do something based on the people they work with, the standards they hold, and the energy exchange between and amongst them to accomplish a goal. When we're looking at an organization's culture and its impact on remote employee burnout, the culture and internal mindset on how work is approached can help us understand where the problems of burnout and workplace stress stem from. For example, does your culture pride itself on constantly achieving, doing and going for the next goal? Or does your culture encourage taking time to reflect and slowing down when needing to strategize so that teams are promoted to work in ebbs and flows?

Ebbs and flows are a natural cycle on this planet, from how the world spins to how the seasons change and animals hibernate. Flowers can't bloom all year round, so why do some organizations expect their teams to perform at 100 per cent all day, every day? By no means am I saying that performance must suffer if we want to create healthy remote teams. Organizations can create both – a team that works from a resilient and healthy place and performs to a high standard. After all, most of us have been programmed so heavily to believe that we constantly have to go, go, go and if you have a handful of leaders that live and breathe this 'hustle and bustle' mentality within an organization, your culture is going to be impacted. But how much of our success comes from 'doing' all the time? Do we attribute our accomplishments to the moments where we slow down, process and integrate our learnings?

The impact of the hustle that starts from the top

The hustle culture promotes careers as such a high priority in its employees' lives that other aspects of being human – such as hobbies, family time and self-care – often take a back seat. So when leaders actively engage in the hustle culture, they are leading by example and unconsciously or sometimes consciously telling their team members to do the same. If the hustle mentality is valued, it becomes what is expected. What is expected and accepted by leaders in your workplace shapes your culture. There is, of course, a mental impact from participating in the hustle culture. It creates a lack of psychological safety in employees regarding taking breaks, sustainably approaching their work, and tending to other priorities outside of work. Employees often feel that they have to be constantly 'on', and the fear can build up so much that they worry that they'll lose their job if they miss something. Hustle culture fosters ongoing toxicity in that if you spend too much time on anything non-work-related, you feel guilty. You cannot let work overrule your downtime, home life and efforts to keep a balanced work–life schedule.

To demonstrate this, let me tell you a story of a client I worked with in the past.

A client of mine approached me, concerned that his organization was losing team members to stress and burnout. This client was at a loss; he was not only losing projects and money, but he was also losing some of his best resources – his team. The situation wasn't positive. A considerable number of his team members were taking stress leave and those who stayed working through this stress were making poor decisions, duplicating efforts and making mistakes.

This concern was keeping him awake at night. He tossed and turned, not knowing what he should and shouldn't do. He wondered why the yoga workshops and the meditation classes he offered on Zoom weren't working. He knew he couldn't just pretend everything was okay anymore. He had to face the facts and deal with this problem from the root, in order to put a stop to it. So when he contacted me, he was committed to resolving this issue once and for all.

We worked together on a one-on-one coaching level not only to address but also to mitigate this massive risk within his team. As an accredited coach who has worked with many founders experiencing the same challenges, I knew what conversations we needed to have first. Knowing how important it is to lead by example, especially for a founder or senior leader, we needed to first focus on him.

Quickly we discovered that he himself was burnt out and, as a founder, his burnt-out approach was causing much of the tension and stress within his team. He had gone so far away from his passion for starting a business that he didn't even know why he was doing it anymore.

He valued things like family, freedom, growth, and work–life balance, and that's why he had decided to work for himself. And here he was years later, not aligned to or living up to any of those values. He was stressed, overworked, overwhelmed, without any time for himself or his beautiful family.

My first objective was to get this founder back to feeling good within himself, reduce his stress and help him create more sustainable working conditions on a personal level. After all, when his nervous system was calm and he was less stressed, he'd be able to see the problem through a different lens – a realistic, calm and committed one. From my experience, I knew that this type of work would have a trickle-down effect on the culture of the team. We worked on areas like his mindset to help him 'let go' of control and to trust his team. We set healthy boundaries for him so he was able to prioritize and find meaning outside of his work. We helped him improve his leadership communication skills so he could more effectively delegate and communicate his expectations.

Over a couple of weeks, the shift in the team began to take place. Because he was happy, content and sustained on the inside, the external world around him started to change, too. He stopped messaging his team out of work hours because he switched off at a normal time in the evening. We created a new time management strategy that incorporated exercise and other activities that made him happy throughout the workweek.

This founder decided to be transparent with his new approaches, sharing his new healthy habits with his team via their messaging channels. This transparency helped promote psychological safety and gave his team 'permission' to do the same. They witnessed him setting respectful boundaries with clients, partners and his team. He hosted a town hall meeting for his team and went through his new strategies, openly addressing burnout and sharing his findings and ways forward. His team started to follow suit and over time, the number of employees taking stress leave reduced and team satisfaction increased. This is the importance of leading by example.

Not all hustles are created equal, but the difference is the mindset in which the hustle is approached within your team. If the mindset is created around achieving all the time with a constant pressure to perform and no time to slow down, this is where issues arise. On the other hand, a team that works extra hard to achieve a common important goal but takes time to slow down and recognize their efforts after a hustle stint is acknowledging the importance of ebbs and flows. You might think that all of this is impossible to achieve within a culture – a team that doesn't experience negative stress loop cycles and achieves its goals to a high standard. So first, let's look at the two extremes of polarity in this case.

Example 1: the hustle culture

The first is the organization with the 'hustle' culture. The senior leaders are constantly connected to Slack and email. They send messages to colleagues all day and night and sometimes even on weekends. Leaders are stressed and exhausted trying to fulfil project oversight responsibilities and have little to no time to connect and communicate with their team members to see how they're doing. Their team members are, of course, following in their managers' footsteps. They worry that if they're seen to take a proper lunch break or decline a meeting at 8 pm, they'll be seen as if they don't care. This hustle organization has been struggling with this type of work environment for a long time. While they are growing their revenues year over year, they're hiring and firing more quickly than they can handle. They convince themselves that people can't keep up with their fast-paced culture and choose to believe that there is something wrong with the people they are hiring instead of looking at their actions as an organization. They won't ask the difficult question, 'What can we do to prevent this?' The team witness their colleagues burning out and taking stress leave, yet it's never addressed in their team meetings. They wonder how much more they can take and convince themselves that after their two-week vacation, maybe something will change. Their culture is built solely on achievement, not effort, and in turn, it's created an unsustainable and unhealthy working environment.

Example 2: the calm and connected culture

The second organization embraces a 'calm and connected' culture. Its team members are clear on their goals and responsibilities and can easily identify how their work contributes to the company's overall success. Workloads and performance are measured based on output and the quality of their work compared to how many hours everyone clocks in each day. Team members thrive in a flexible environment that promotes breaks and deep work time. They feel they can look after their health and perform to a high standard. Leaders regularly take time away from work, switch off at reasonable times in the evenings, and don't work weekends. It's not unusual for leaders to take longer breaks on sunny days and share their wellbeing practices in Slack with their team. Again, team members follow in the footsteps of their leaders and feel safe to take time away from work when they need it. They feel like they have the time and permission to create a balanced work and life schedule, and see an increase in their productivity as a result. This organization is growing its revenues year over year, achieving all its company metrics and successfully retaining its workforce. The teams are innovative and constantly coming up with new ideas and taking responsibility for making continuous improvements. Leaders' satisfaction is high as their team conversations are based around growth rather than trying to help team members feel less stressed. Teams are happy and therefore they are naturally promoting their organization as a great place to work. The company reviews are phenomenal, making it easy to attract ideal candidates.

Changing culture requires changing mindset

So when it comes to changing our culture, what makes for a winning organizational mindset in effecting this healthy and effective change? Carol Dweck, a Stanford psychologist, advocates a growth mindset over a fixed mindset (2007). A growth mindset is when we can continually improve with learning. The growth mindset focuses not just on the results we produce but also on the effort we put into a project or task. In contrast, a fixed mindset believes that we have fixed abilities and skills and that it doesn't matter how much effort we put into something – we will always remain the same. The fixed mindset focuses solely on results and clearly defines whether something is 'good' or 'bad'. It doesn't consider the learnings or the expanded experience gained from trying something new. How this relates to burnout cultures is something I've witnessed repeatedly with my clients. Organizations that suffer from burnout in their teams repeatedly promote a fixed mindset. The fixed mindset culture will start at the top of the organizational chart and say, 'this is just the way we are; we will never change so we need to find people who will resonate with our approach.' A growth mindset culture will look at the problem (in this case employee burnout) and try to learn from it as a company. This fixed and growth mindset approach can trickle down into all business areas, such as performance management. For example, instead of recognizing a team member for trying a new innovative project that produced a lot of key learnings for the organization, leaders with a fixed mindset choose to look only at the results and metrics it impacted.

A growth mindset culture accepts and welcomes learnings and incremental improvements that can lead to more significant changes for the long term. One way growth mindset organizations can actively assess their culture and what their teams need is by collecting data. Sending employee surveys and collecting feedback from qualitative and quantitative perspectives can open up insights and blind spots that may have previously gone unnoticed. It's a robust activity to hear directly from all team members about what they need, want and desire in order to feel happy and healthy in their work. Collecting data regularly can ensure that the organization is measuring the impact of any new projects and strategies on employee wellbeing. It also demonstrates a level of care and commitment from leadership to create a great workplace. When data is pulled on specific areas on a grand scale, it empowers leaders by helping them understand the common threads – both challenges and opportunities. Leaders can take this feedback and create a plan to address the issues. Often leadership teams might identify many problems and areas for improvement, and it can feel overwhelming for organizations to know where to start.

ONE STEP AT A TIME

What is important to remember is that companies don't have to solve everything straight away. Out of 10 issues, leaders might focus on the top three for the next six months. The key to collecting data is to communicate the findings to your team and what the plan of action is moving forward. Doing so creates a trusting environment and ensures that team members will be much more likely to provide candid feedback in the future.

In the first section of this book, The Self, we covered healthy boundaries and how important it is to mitigate burnout and create sustainable, productive teams. Employees can only create healthy boundaries if organizations create safe working environments that promote and respect their employees' boundaries for their mental, emotional and psychological wellbeing.

How organizations can support and promote healthy boundaries

As mentioned in the self section, it's an important life and professional lesson to learn – how we can create and uphold healthy boundaries in our lives and work in order to feel well. In this section, we'll look at the various ways organizations can support healthier ways of working in their teams, like the right to disconnect. Sure, being able to set boundaries and understand the boundaries you need to create on a personal level is important, but all the boundary building in the world won't help your team members all that much if your organization doesn't have a culture and policies that support their efforts.

Organizations need to adapt their culture to an environment that promotes vacations, breaks from work and the right to disconnect just as much as they promote achievement, results and hard work. Many areas that we cover in this book support organizations in promoting and helping their teams maintain healthy boundaries, from leadership leading by example to creating more flexible remote communication processes. This leads to overall happier and healthier remote teams. Some organizations promote healthy boundaries by introducing incentives like meeting-free days or even communication-free afternoons for all their employees, company-wide. Doing so provides a statement to the workforce that, on an organizational level, leaders understand that there's more to work than just doing, executing and being in constant communication.

Organizations that have resisted promoting this new and healthier approach to work are now being forced to revisit how healthy their connectivity expectations are for their team members.

The right to disconnect

Legislation worldwide is now holding organizations accountable to healthier working environments through a mandate known as the Right To Disconnect. The concept of 'right to disconnect' emerged in France in 2017 as part of a new set of labour laws (Boring, 2020). This law mandates that employers with 50 or more employees have a policy that addresses the use of smartphones.

As a relatively new concept, there are differing interpretations of what a 'right to disconnect' is. In general, it is the concept that workers should be able to disconnect from workplace communications channels outside of working hours. The right to disconnect allows workers to disengage from their work and not receive or answer work-related emails, calls or messages outside of regular working hours.

Some have argued a right to disconnect is a way to ensure a balance between work and private life. Cognitive and emotional overload from 'hyper-connectivity' has been noted to have negative effects (Ginès i Fabrellas, 2019), including a sense of fatigue due to the 'psychosocial risk' of being constantly connected.

According to Statistics Canada (StatCan), up to 40 per cent of Canadians have worked from home due to pandemic restrictions (Mehdi and Morissette, 2021). This is in contrast to only about 8 per cent of workers working any of their scheduled hours from home in 2018. Workers said that they are largely pleased with their new teleworking arrangements; however, problems 'switching off' at the end of the day have been the most reported concern.

For organizations to fully embrace and adopt the right to disconnect, it requires more than just a standard policy uploaded to a company web page. To create an environment for employees to feel safe to disconnect from work, we have to look at our culture and our processes. Both must support the healthy boundaries teams create around fully disconnecting from work.

For example, an organization might promote disconnection after work hours. Still, if an employee feels increased pressure from their manager, who continually pings them and sends them messages outside of work hours, they may feel the right to disconnect doesn't apply to them. Remote teams need to feel psychologically safe in their ability to disconnect from their work – that in doing so, their position, future opportunities and even likeability won't be compromised.

So while we can create policies around this legislation, which varies across countries, it's essential to ask, 'How deep is the right to disconnect embedded into our culture?' Are leaders equipped to understand how their blind spots or biases can compromise internal policies? Do they understand how their actions can prevent team members from fully disconnecting, and have they revisited their expectations around their team's working hours and availability?

To truly embrace the right to disconnect, we have to activate this mindset throughout our workforce, and continually seek to understand the processes and procedures that can improve working environments so people feel even more supported in disconnecting fully from their work.

The impact of purpose-driven work

Now more than ever, companies need to create common threads within the organization that can unite teams, regardless of their dispersed physical locations. It's an organization's responsibility to help employees understand and believe in why their work matters.

Studies show that when people believe that their work matters, they're four times more likely to be engaged, are more motivated, learn faster, and are more fulfilled (Science of Purpose, nd).

Research shows that philanthropic giving and having a purposeful mission can boost your physical and mental health (Cleveland Clinic, 2020). Health benefits associated with giving can include lower blood pressure, increased self-esteem, less depression and lower stress levels. One of the keys to unlocking lower stress levels amongst teams could be creating a purpose-driven organization.

Not only do we see health benefits associated with giving back, but we also find a reduction in employee turnover. Recent studies show that there is a 50 per cent reduction in employee turnover when employees are engaged in corporate social responsibility (CSR) programmes (Adamson and Barnes, 2021). A PwC survey of over 502 leaders revealed that while 79 per cent of leaders think that connecting their people to an inspiring purpose is critical to success, just 27 per cent say they regularly enact purpose when working with their teams (Schuyler, 2016).

Purpose does more than just help you tell a unique story for your team and customers. It raises the level of conscious awareness within an organization and its teams. Closing the gap between the stimulating idea of purpose and its transformative practice to drive employee engagement, motivation, and fulfilment may be the key to remote teams' challenges. It shines a light on a business's evolutionary path. It creates an awareness greater than company key performance indicators (KPIs) and objectives and key results (OKRs). It empowers employees, customers and leaders to embody a greater perspective on the world itself and connect all stakeholders through a shared vision of being and doing better.

Now more than ever before, remote teams need a reason more significant than their current situation to keep going in challenging times.

Benefits of purpose-driven cultures

The future of work is sure to include a mixture of remote and hybrid working environments. Even in these cases, organizations need to pay careful attention to the new norms and culture they're creating – they're actively building the glue that binds their people together.

The ripple effect is that charity programmes also help to create purpose-driven company cultures focused on answering the 'why'. This can pave the way for noticeable improvements in employee engagement, attraction and retention. Setting out to solve big problems brings a sense of purpose and meaning to your work and life. And when people have a cause big enough, they can move mountains. That's the power of a massively transformative purpose. It enrols people you haven't even met. Why? Because instead of watching events unfold and feeling powerless, we feel like we can make a difference, that our efforts matter.

But, in case you need even more research and insights into why your team should embrace a purpose-driven culture and how it can support you in managing and reducing burnout in your team, here are three research-based benefits to show you the positive effect that doing this work will have on your team.

1 *Engage employees, which leads to better performance overall.* If a company culture is positive, it should motivate employees regardless of where they are located, what they do in their jobs or how much adversity they face. When employees can see how their work contributes to others and serves a more significant reason, research shows they become better, and more engaged in their work (Luturlean et al, 2019). Providing teams with the opportunity to do work that feels fulfilling and meaningful to them can support them in feeling better within their work. Great culture is the rocket fuel your team needs to propel them forward in achieving their goals and ensure they are happy and well along the way.

2 *Create an environment of innovation and excitement.* When you provide people with a 'WHY' they tend to think 'bigger picture'. It starts by creating a culture of excitement about why you're doing what you're doing. Studies show that when we think about our impact on others or directly help someone else, we get a boost of the 'happiness trifecta' of neurotransmitters: oxytocin, dopamine, and serotonin (Luturlean et al, 2019). Oxytocin supports empathy

and social bonding (Ritvo, 2014). Dopamine plays a significant role in motivation, wellbeing and movement, resulting in increased engagement, motivation and innovation.

3 *Speak a common language amongst all employees.* It doesn't matter where you come from, what your native language is, or what department you work in when you have a culture that's embraced – everyone shows up for themselves, each other and external stakeholders in the same way. It can help create a sense of trust within a team and thus leads to more supportive environments. Having a shared purpose ensures your team has a clear, contribution-focused purpose statement to harmonize energy (Luturlean et al, 2019), and that purpose can articulate it at all levels (Jouany, 2019). There's certain attitudes, behaviours and values that are non-negotiables in anything that you do at work.

Future generational values

How is your organization preparing to align with upcoming generational values and motivations? If companies want to attract the best talent, they have to create an inspiring and relatable place to work. The newest up-and-coming talent is Generation Z, people born between 1997 and 2012. Gen Z comprises roughly 33 per cent of the world's population and is projected to overtake Millennials in sheer numbers in 2022 (Spitznagel, 2020). So from an employer perspective, it's fundamental to understand what Gen Z cares about, their motivations in their work, and their expectations from their future employers. Gen Z's passion lies in effecting positive change. The 2019 Porter Novelli/Cone Gen Z Purpose Study found that Gen Z-ers are primarily concerned about the health of our planet (87 per cent), and care deeply about social and environmental issues (88 per cent).

With work and life more combined now than ever, no longer can we separate our value system between the work that we do and the lives that we live. Gen Z-ers aren't settling for any less. In a recent study by Girls With Impact, fully 45 per cent of Gen Z want to work for a company that makes a positive difference in the world (2019).

So how can companies be the place Gen Z and other generations want to work? The pay cheque is essential, but the purpose is critical. With more than half the world working remotely, organizations need to go above and beyond to align to this generation's values and motives, and create a meaningful purpose in a remote working environment. Gen Z seek purpose in their work at a much higher rate than previous generations, and they require that purpose to be meaningful.

No longer is it acceptable for organizations to create a mission statement and a value checklist that isn't genuinely activated within their teams. Having a deeply embedded purpose at the core of all of the company's objectives ensures that company culture becomes a living, breathing and truly active mindset that's a part of every working day. Organizations are required to dig deep and to create a purpose that stems from the values and motives of their team and employees. Only then can we genuinely attract and retain future generations and create happier, engaged and more committed teams.

Flexible work patterns

The four-day workweek has grown in popularity over recent years, and many companies are choosing to adopt and redefine the five days a week, 9 to 5 model. New structures like this have us all questioning – 'Is the 9 to 5 model outdated?'

Perpetual Guardian, a New Zealand firm, trialled a four-day week. A survey of employees found that 78 per cent could more effectively balance their work and home life (Booth, 2019), compared to 54 per cent prior to the experiment. In Iceland, the four-day workweek was trialed by the Reykjavík City Council and the national government (BBC News, 2021). The trial included more than 2,500 workers, which amounts to about 1 per cent of Iceland's working population between 2015 and 2019. They found that, after this trial, workers reported feeling less stressed and at risk of burnout, and said their health and work–life balance had improved. They also reported having more time to spend with their families, do hobbies and complete household chores.

This level of flexibility throughout the workday can support employees in creating a better work–life integration and prioritize the habits, practices and activities outside of work that help them feel well and happy. The research shows us that when employees can invest energy in areas that support their wellbeing, they can be up to four times less likely to feel burnout at work (Plemons, 2018). Research also indicates that offering flexible work increases job satisfaction and lowers burnout (Howington, nd).

Introducing more flexibility into the workplace can feel like a daunting task for any leadership team, and it does have multiple layers of consideration to it. Flexibility can be introduced in stages and will look different for every department and, in some cases, every team. For example, if you have a customer service department supporting customers on the phone or chatting at a specific time, your workforce planning can't allow for flexibility. However, for your engineering department that primarily isn't customer-facing, it might make sense to consider how flexibility can be introduced into this type of environment.

Suppose a four-day workweek seems very far away from your organization's current situation. In that case, I invite you to consider introducing micro ways of flexible working to your team members – for example, creating flexibility around start and end times to a particular day and introducing 'core hours' into your team. Core hours are the main hours that your team are required to be online at the same time together. Outside of these core hours, team members can choose to start between specific hours in the morning; the time they finish work will depend on when they start.

Wellness is not the answer

Wellness in the workplace is an $8 billion industry in the United States, and forward-thinking workplaces may think they are doing a great service by offering yoga, meditation classes, and other wellness services. But research reveals that those efforts are not working. A 2019 Harvard Medical School study shows that workplace wellness programmes had no impact on overall health, sleep quality, nutrition choices, health markers, or health care usage, failing to move the needle on the very issues that they claimed to redress (Song and Baicker, 2019). The programmes also failed to improve basic workplace metrics such as absenteeism, performance quality, and retention of key employees.

The current spend on wellness is not fixing the problems it targets. So what can? First, we must broaden our definition of wellness and understand that wellness is created from the daily environments we create for our teams. If we have processes that empower us to have the time and safety to schedule wellness activities throughout our workday, it doesn't necessarily matter what wellness activities we actually 'do'. For remote team members to have this time and safety to live wellness in their working environments, we must revisit our organizational processes and structures.

References

Adamson, C and Barnes, K (2021) Building the business case for social responsibility, *Your Cause from Blackbaud*, 10 November, https://solutions.yourcause.com/building-the-business-case-for-social-responsibility (archived at https://perma.cc/MT62-Y74H)

Aggarwal, A and Rozwell, C (2018) Make your digital workplace employee-friendly with these six IoT best practices, *Gartner.com*, 20 August, www.gartner.com/en/documents/3887664 (archived at https://perma.cc/N9XQ-DKQQ)

BBC News (2021) Four-day week 'an overwhelming success' in Iceland, *Business*, 6 July, www.bbc.com/news/business-57724779 (archived at https://perma.cc/RGA7-8Z2K)

Booth, R (2019) Four-day week: trial finds lower stress and increased productivity, *The Guardian*, 19 February, www.theguardian.com/money/2019/feb/19/four-day-week-trial-study-finds-lower-stress-but-no-cut-in-output (archived at https://perma.cc/N4JT-389Q)

Boring, N (2020) Telework and the French 'right to disconnect', *Library of Congress*, 21 August, https://blogs.loc.gov/law/2020/08/telework-and-the-french-right-to-disconnect (archived at https://perma.cc/8KSZ-JHPB)

Cielo (nd) Infographic: The impact of remote working on talent acquisition, www. cielotalent.com/insights/infographic-the-impact-of-remote-working-on-talent-acquisition (archived at https://perma.cc/GFG7-N9M3)

Cleveland Clinic (2020) Why giving is good for your health: Studies show how giving affects your body, *Cleveland Clinic Health Essentials*, 28 October, https://health.clevelandclinic.org/why-giving-is-good-for-your-health (archived at https://perma.cc/V9L4-S7WS)

Dweck, C S (2007) *Mindset: The new psychology of success*, Ballantine Books, New York

Ginès i Fabrellas, A (2019) Are new technologies threatening employee well-being? *Do Better by Esade*, 21 October, https://dobetter.esade.edu/en/new-technologies-employees (archived at https://perma.cc/VKP5-78Q3)

Girls with Impact (2019) What's inside the minds of Gen Z: A special report, www. girlswithimpact.org/genz (archived at https://perma.cc/XC92-TDCE)

Glassdoor (2020) The ROI of employer branding, *Glassdoor for Employers*, 31 August, www.glassdoor.com/employers/blog/the-roi-of-employer-branding (archived at https://perma.cc/TS7F-QJ6N)

Howington, J (nd) Flexible work increases job satisfaction and lowers burnout, study confirms, *Flexjobs*, www.flexjobs.com/blog/post/flexible-work-increases-job-satisfaction-and-lowers-burnout-study-confirms (archived at https://perma.cc/EH68-MWJC)

HR Daily Advisor (2019) Over one-third of employees will be job hunting in 2019, https://hrdailyadvisor.blr.com/2019/03/13/over-one-third-of-employees-will-be-job-hunting-in-2019/ (archived at https://perma.cc/F4XH-DGHK)

Jouany, V (2019) Internal communications: How to align employees with your strategic goals? Haiilo, https://blog.smarp.com/internal-communications-how-to-align-employees-with-your-strategic-goals (archived at https://perma.cc/6EEX-4ZT8)

Luturlean, B S, Prasetio, A P and Saragih, R (2019). The effect of human resource practice, perceived organizational support and work–life balance in enhancing employee's affective commitment, *Journal of Management and Marketing Review*, 4 (4) pp 242–53

Lynch, S (2015) Why your workplace might be killing you, Stanford Graduate School of Business, 23 February, www.gsb.stanford.edu/insights/why-your-workplace-might-be-killing-you (archived at https://perma.cc/SU3A-HXZE)

Mehdi, T and Morissette, R (2021) Working from home in Canada: What have we learned so far? *Statistics Canada*, 27 October, www150.statcan.gc.ca/n1/pub/36-28-0001/2021010/article/00001-eng.htm (archived at https://perma.cc/S9E5-XL74)

Microsoft (2022) Work Trend Index, www.microsoft.com/en-us/worklab/work-trend-index/great-expectations-making-hybrid-work-work (archived at https://perma.cc/58L3-UDBQ)

Moneypenny (2022) UK's attitudes to switching jobs in 2022, 23 February, www.moneypenny.com/uk/resources/blog/uks-attitudes-to-switching-jobs-in-2022-moneypenny (archived at https://perma.cc/9USS-F48L)

Pelta, R (2021) FlexJobs survey finds employees want remote work post-pandemic, *Flexjobs*, www.flexjobs.com/blog/post/flexjobs-survey-finds-employees-want-remote-work-post-pandemic (archived at https://perma.cc/Y4N2-P83G)

Plemons, J (2018) 2 Remedies for reducing burnout among healthcare workers, *Gallup Workplace*, 13 March, www.gallup.com/workplace/236132/remedies-reducing-burnout-among-healthcare-workers.aspx (archived at https://perma.cc/XG4B-WSHL)

Porter Novelli/Cone (2019) Porter Novelli/Cone Gen Z purpose study, www.conecomm.com/research-blog/cone-gen-z-purpose-study (archived at https://perma.cc/LD5Y-4MSH)

Prudential (2021) Increasingly, workers expect pandemic workplace adaptations to stick, *Prudential Newsroom*, 6 April, https://news.prudential.com/increasingly-workers-expect-pandemic-workplace-adaptations-to-stick.htm (archived at https://perma.cc/F2T5-FXYE)

Richards, K (nd) How your leadership style affects your ability to recruit and retain employees, *Inc*, www.inc.com/kelli-richards/how-your-leadership-style-affects-your-ability-to-.html (archived at https://perma.cc/X7F7-435T)

Ritvo, E (2014) The neuroscience of giving: Proof that helping others helps you, *Psychology Today*, 24 April, www.psychologytoday.com/us/blog/vitality/201404/the-neuroscience-giving (archived at https://perma.cc/5QUZ-AG64)

Schuyler, S (2017) Putting purpose to work: A study of purpose in the workplace, *PricewaterhouseCoopers*, www.pwc.com/us/en/purpose-workplace-study.html (archived at https://perma.cc/6XY5-4F5X)

Science of Purpose (nd) http://scienceofpurpose.org (archived at https://perma.cc/M5NP-HRX5)

Song, Z and Baicker, K (2019) Effect of a workplace wellness program on employee health and economic outcomes, *Journal of the American Medical Association*, 16 April, https://jamanetwork.com/journals/jama/fullarticle/2730614 (archived at https://perma.cc/2QMJ-SPGL)

Spitznagel, E (2020) Generation Z is bigger than millennials – and they're out to change the world, *New York Post*, 25 January, https://nypost.com/2020/01/25/generation-z-is-bigger-than-millennials-and-theyre-out-to-change-the-world (archived at https://perma.cc/4QDQ-235H)

WHO (nd) Mental health in the workplace, www.who.int/teams/mental-health-and-substance-use/promotion-prevention/mental-health-in-the-workplace (archived at https://perma.cc/A7FW-8FLP)

07

Remote-first processes

How much of an impact do internal company processes like communication have on employees' wellbeing and the likelihood of burning out?

In 2021, Wakefield Research found that 89 per cent of employees said daily work tasks such as sorting through an inbox of unopened emails or navigating incoming Slack or Teams messages were amongst the most unpleasant parts of working remotely (Vohra, 2021). Additionally, 38 per cent said this 'email fatigue' was likely to push them to quit their jobs, and 51 per cent listed the volume of emails and Slack or Teams messages they received as a top reason why they'd consider leaving their jobs.

Constant meetings, overwhelming seas of notifications and endless emails require teams to be active, available and responsive for most of their workday. In a study, The Webcam Survey: Exhausted or Engaged, nearly half of US professionals working remotely (49 per cent), which translates to 32 million individuals, reported a high degree of exhaustion as a direct result of numerous daily video calls (Virtira, 2021). Referred to as 'Zoom fatigue', the exhaustion stems from a combination of increased meetings and the pressure to have webcams on for all of them. The back-to-back meeting culture has resulted in workers struggling to get a five-minute break between calls and experiencing 'Zoom fatigue' as part and parcel of working remotely. How has this standard of working come to be accepted in today's climate? The benefits of being so connected through technology can easily translate into our biggest personal challenges.

The difference between companies that succeed at their remote team processes and those that don't lies in their openness and ability to create new processes based around how a remote team operates remote-first processes. Where friction occurs is when organizations try to replicate office environments into virtually distributed teams – usually not the best strategy.

What is a remote-first process?

Remote-first, also known as digital-first and virtual-first, is built upon the basis that teams are virtually distributed. So let's start by defining what a remote-first process is. Remote-first means something is built and optimized for your remote teams' environment first. If you're working in a hybrid team environment, focusing on remote-first internal processes means you consider how it will work for office teams as secondary.

In a remote-first team, processes are built from the ground up with the assumption that not everyone is face-to-face, or even in the same time zone. Some of the most successful remote teams like Basecamp (2022), GitLab (nd), and Buffer (Griffis, 2018) spend time and resources constantly improving their internal remote-first processes. This includes how their remote team communicates, how projects are managed, how promotions are given, and how performance is measured. Without these considerations, teams aren't working remotely in an optimized way, which increases bottlenecks like too many meetings and endless chaotic communication.

Everything your team does throughout their workday makes up processes that companies should optimize for a remote team environment. Remote organizations that don't create or optimize their strategies for remote team environments aren't able to operate fully effectively.

Why remote-first matters in reducing burnout

In my experience in working with dozens of organizations, I've found that a lack of remote-first processes contributes significantly to employee burnout. Remote-first processes produce and promote greater work–life balance. For example, consider teams focused too much on meetings (synchronous communication). Their teams are stuck all day in online discussions, feeling fatigued. In addition, they have to work extra hours to catch up on the work that came as a result of the meetings. I see teams exhausted and unmotivated due to not having the time or space for creative, productive work. Without this time for deep work and uninterrupted focus in our calendars, we don't have time to think proactively, to plan or to replenish ourselves when we need to. Teams working in this way often don't have time to just 'be'.

To take this one step further, many teams in this situation often don't take breaks. That means they have no time for a healthy lunch, a walk outside in the fresh air or even a couple of minutes to just breathe. A lack of remote-first communication can play havoc with our team members' nervous systems and stress response. Over weeks and even months, this havoc will eventually lead to an entire system shut down – burnout.

Remote first = flexibility in process + productivity
based on output + less reactivity

Remote-first reduces proximity bias in hybrid teams

As mentioned earlier, proximity bias is the idea that team members with close physical proximity to their team and company leaders will be perceived as better workers and ultimately find more success in the workplace than their remote counterparts (Moran, 2021). When there is a lack of remote-first processes, hybrid teams tend to have meetings based around an office-centric environment.

In that environment, remote team members have to join meetings virtually while everyone else is in one room together. This type of process puts remote team members on the back burner – the playing field isn't level, and it's more challenging to speak up, give feedback and feel included. Remote-first processes combat that, level the playing field, and ensure everyone feels included.

One of the most fundamental aspects of building a thriving remote organization is creating and improving remote-first processes. All internal operations are optimized for remote and flexible environments by remote-first methods. Processes like:

- How we communicate flexibly as opposed to requiring real-time meetings (which isn't sustainable, especially at scale. More people and projects equals more meetings).
- How we manage and share information in written form as opposed to having to verbally communicate (which isn't scalable).
- How we manage performance by the quality of output as opposed to the number of hours our teams work (which isn't flexible).
- How we equip leaders and employees with the tools and knowledge to develop enough self-awareness that they can manage their wellbeing and maintain boundaries as opposed to burning out (which isn't healthy).

Communication

Communication is at the core of every team. How we communicate determines our success in maintaining team engagement, wellbeing and even effectiveness. Anderson et al (2007) conclude that one of the key challenges for effective facilitation of virtual teams is ensuring clear communication amongst team members. Dow and Taylor (2008) define communication as a leading factor for virtual teams to ensure team members, managers and stakeholders are informed and on track to pursue the project objectives. Communication is also the key to identifying issues, risks, misunderstandings, and all other challenges to project completion.

Effective communication builds trust and relationships

Trust within virtual teams is closely linked to communication, and is an important dynamic in nearly every model of knowledge sharing in virtual teams (Keyzerman, 2003). Research has shown that people build trust more easily with those they meet in person than with those they meet only electronically. With little or no face-to-face dialogue, then, it can be difficult for virtual teams to foster personal relationships, and this magnifies trust issues (Lerner, 2008). Duarte and Snyder (2000) found that if multiple languages and diverse cultures are added, it becomes even more difficult to create and build trust amongst individuals and teams.

To overcome these challenges and avoid ambiguity and misunderstanding, virtual teams need to ensure that their communication is accurate, precise and simple (Lee-Kelley et al, 2004). Based on their research, Oertig and Buergi (2006) recommend that members of cross-cultural teams pay attention to the pace of their speech, the use of slang, and different accents. For example, the same word can have different meanings in different languages – in Japanese culture, 'yes' can mean 'I will think about it' rather than 'I agree'. In addition, diverse teams need to apply cultural intelligence and make a point of communicating respect for differences amongst team members (Brake, 2006). Additionally, these teams should provide opportunities for members to dialogue about the differences and learn from one another.

The types of remote team communication

So where do we begin? What should we work on improving first in our remote-first process? To start, let's look at communication. There are two significant methods of communication that every remote or hybrid team should consider. For teams to effectively communicate and be successful, team members must adopt varied ways of communicating in both real time (synchronous) and delayed time (asynchronous) through communication tools and technology. Globally dispersed teams inevitably require team members to work across various time zones. Asynchronous communication tools allow team members to interact together, but due to differences in 'daylight' or 'working hours' amongst team members, time-sensitive projects can suffer from the delays in response.

1 **Synchronous** communication is when we communicate in real time, e.g. conducting a meeting or having a phone call.

2 **Asynchronous** communication is when we communicate with each other in delayed time, e.g. when we use a messaging tool or send an email and wait for a response.

The challenge for many remote organizations is that they focus too heavily on synchronous communication because this is the way most of us worked up until the remote revolution. In an office setting, team members would come into a building and perform a set shift, collaborating together when they were all there in person. When they left after 5 pm, they wouldn't resume or connect again until the following working day.

This way of working that the office environment is created on has been around since the industrial revolution. The standard 9 to 5 and in-person meeting culture was created around the expectation that people would be working in the same location together, so it makes sense that it won't necessarily translate into the perfect process for remote teams that work in a completely different way.

However, many organizations try to replicate office processes in the remote environment, forcing it to work, resulting in friction such as an overwhelming number of meetings and ineffective collaboration both in and between teams. Remote organizations must revisit their beliefs and standards around how they work with an open mindset and a sense of curiosity. Of course, synchronous communication and collaboration are essential for every team. Still, that doesn't mean it's the only working mode that exists, and it doesn't imply that it's always the best way for remote teams to work.

Synchronous communication

The first step for any organization is to take a realistic and clear look at its current meeting culture. Many meetings are ineffective and not the best use of everyone's time. The University of North Carolina surveyed 182 senior managers in various industries and 65 per cent said meetings keep them from completing their work, 71 per cent said meetings are unproductive and inefficient, and 64 per cent said meetings come at the expense of deep thinking (Gourani, 2021). Someone probably created the term 'meeting about a meeting' to add humour to a situation that was incredibly frustrating. It's true that many organizations aren't proactively measuring the effectiveness of the meetings being conducted within their teams.

When organizations hold too many poorly planned meetings, the organizational culture begins to place little value or importance on everyone's time. This translates into meetings that don't have a clear agenda or objective, and sees meeting participants from various teams being invited without careful consideration of whether they even need to be there. When clear agendas and action points are not outlined ahead of time, it's guaranteed that the meeting discussion will branch into various topics and often become irrelevant to the reason the meeting was set up in the first place. This can lead to meetings running over time, requiring participants to stay on longer than they expected. That extra time can eat into participants' breaks or time allocated for deep work, or has them running late for the next meeting, which continues the cycle of being delayed again and again throughout their day.

This is not to say that meetings aren't important in remote teams – we don't want to eliminate the opportunity to see our team members on a video call altogether. In fact, meetings are fundamental to the success of remote teams, but they need to be of high quality. Plazas (2013) found that virtual team members lack the opportunity to read each others' body language, a large part of effective communication, and rely on video conferencing for this. In addition, relying on reading or interpreting a written text can lead to many challenges amongst individuals and teams, including possibly creating and heightening conflict issues.

You might have found yourself in a similar position once or twice before. You might be nodding your head in agreement. How often do you experience this type of stress in your working week right now? I call it stress because it is taking a toll on our nervous systems and sending us into flight or fight mode. Racing from Zoom call to Zoom call without the decisions or discussions that actually needed to happen is frustrating. It's frustrating because there is a lack of value placed on everyone's time.

Organizations measure productivity and metrics and KPIs but fail to take the time to measure the effectiveness of their meetings. Creating, hosting or setting up a meeting is usually open for interpretation and companies don't take the time to create a set of standards and best practices across their teams.

While one meeting participant or facilitator might make the commitment to strive to create better meetings in their company, without the effort of everyone, it's impossible to make the significant improvements needed. Everyone in the organization needs to acknowledge the WHY behind running better meetings and share responsibility for making them better.

As a challenge, I invite you to look at your calendar where all your meetings are logged. Over the past four weeks, how many of those meetings did you really need to be at? How many of those meetings would you rate as effective? How many had an agenda? How many did you actively participate in? How many ran over time? How many needed to be the duration they originally were set for?

We can all make improvements and changes to our meetings that can help us create more space and time within our day, but the effort of one person alone isn't enough to change the way a whole company works.

You can use the following checklist at least every quarter to ensure you're spending your time and energy wisely and that you:

- have meaningful meetings that are of value;
- have enough time and flexibility in your days to do deep work;
- are communicating in the most effective ways possible;
- are not wasting time attending meetings that are not relevant to you.

One-on-one meetings

Review your recurring one-on-one meetings and ask yourself:

- Do you need to have this meeting? What's the value of this meeting for both parties?

- Can the cadence of this meeting be changed? For example, once a month, every two weeks, every six weeks?
- Can the duration of this meeting be changed? For example, 45 minutes instead of 60?
- Is this meeting at a convenient time for both participants?

Team meetings

Review your team's recurring meetings and ask yourself:

- What's the value of this meeting? Are we aligned as a group on the purpose and value of this meeting, or do we need to revisit this together?
- How is this discussion contributing to our goal?
- What's the desired outcome?
- Does this meeting have an agenda each week? If not, who should take responsibility for this agenda?
- Does this meeting have a set of action items each week that includes a clear ask from all participants?
- Do I need to be at this meeting or is there someone else in my department who is attending and can fill me in afterwards?
- Do we clearly summarize the discussion of the meeting and take notes on the next steps to inform the next agenda? If not, who can take responsibility for that?
- Can we reduce the length of time we spend in this meeting? What would make sense?
- How about the cadence? Do we need to have this meeting as often as we do?

Getting team-wide buy-in

The first step is to create a case for why it's important to improve and reduce ineffective meetings. In order to get everyone bought into the idea, everyone needs a reason WHY. The first part of that why is around the data. Many people will think in terms of metrics, money and numbers, so appealing to the logical side of the organization culture means building a case on the cost of meetings. **What are meetings costing the organization every year? What are ineffective meetings costing the organization every year?** It can be challenging to establish these metrics because the data is both qualitative (how your team feels about meetings) and quantitative (for example, how much of your team's time is spent in meetings).

Once the data is collected, as an organization you should have a clear numerical indicator as to the importance of effective meetings and the cost of ineffective meetings. The second part is to understand how improving the standard of meetings within your organization relates to and promotes your company culture. Often organizations have a clear set of values, principles and/or behaviours to guide team members in how they work and interact with each other and their clients. Your effort to improve meetings should align with established values, principles and/or behaviours.

> For example, a value you might have is to provide everyone with the opportunity to be creative and to do their very best work, and you see that ineffective meetings have gotten in the way of this. Ineffective meetings result in a lack of time for creativity, which goes against the guiding principles of your organization. In order to support and empower your team to be even more creative, you rally everyone together to discuss the impact of the current meeting culture on employee creativity. Propose the best practices and standards that can support everyone in having only highly productive meetings that respect the use of everyone's time.

In approaching this from a culture and data perspective, as an organization, you're ensuring a strong sense of responsibility amongst the team because, after all, the success of improving meetings is the responsibility of everyone within the organization, not just any one or two individuals. In order to generate that sense of responsibility amongst the team, we have to understand the various motivations of our team members. For some, it's around saving time, reducing costs and improving metrics. Others may be motivated by the promise of more time to do their work, and how that time can allow them to do more purposeful or creative work or even enable deeper collaboration.

Mapping out your plan of action

Now that you have a strong case for the WHY, the next step is to map out your plan of action as to how you can create these shared best practices for your team.

Of course, you could choose to create a list of best practices and send it out to everyone within your organization to read, but if you want to create a culture of shared responsibility, it's important to get your team involved in the creation process and to hear their feedback, ideas and thoughts. In my experience, when a team is involved in creating the best practices themselves in a team environment, members are much more likely to take responsibility for what was agreed upon.

This process shifts the culture from a 'here's what we need you to do' to a 'let's do this all together so we can help each other and get better as a team'. It shifts the focus from 'I' to 'we' and helps teams understand that improvements are created when everyone takes part. It promotes active participation in the continual improvement of how the team functions and helps members feel valued and that you are listening to what they have to say. This is the type of organizational mindset we want in our remote teams – one where everyone understands their efforts and how they contribute to the overall success of the team. They also know their efforts will not only benefit them as individuals but the team as a whole.

How you create your team's meeting best practices guide/playbook/guidelines (call it what you wish) depends on the number of employees you have and, of course, the resources you have to conduct this project. As a reminder, it can be tempting to think that a project like this can take up too much time, or that your organization can't possibly dedicate the resources to doing something like this. In these cases, where you might struggle for 'buy-in' from yourself or even other members of your leadership team, it's important to revert back to the bigger-picture WHY. If you've collected metrics and data as to the cost and implications of poor-quality meetings, it'll be much easier for you and your team to give this improvement project the time and attention that it deserves.

If you have a smaller team headcount, you can probably conduct a discussion- and activity-based meeting around this with everyone. If you have a larger organization, you might decide to involve only your leadership teams for now and divide that group into smaller cohorts where you can run this type of activity.

To start the activity, it's important to highlight where your organization is in relation to meetings and communicate the WHY with the rest of the team (metrics and culture). Next you might decide to deliver some training on effective meetings (if you'd like access to training on effective remote team meetings go to www.operateremote.com/book). Within this training part, you might showcase some of the best practices on meetings I've listed below. The final and most important point of this activity is to get your team to reflect on meetings and contribute their thoughts to the best practices guides. To do this, I recommend the following template:

- START: What should we as a team start doing to improve meetings remotely?

- STOP: What should we as a team stop doing to improve meetings remotely?

- CONTINUE: What should we as a team continue doing to improve meetings remotely?

Finally, with this activity, I recommend you use a tool that allows everyone to input their answers in text form. While you might be tempted to discuss this with everyone, we want to ensure we're valuing time and giving everyone the opportunity to share their thoughts. To do this, you might choose to use a whiteboard tool like Miro, a spreadsheet that everyone has access to (Google Sheets, Excel, etc.) or a collaboration tool (Parabol.co is my personal favourite).

After everyone has had the opportunity to summarize their thoughts under the headings STOP, START and CONTINUE, you might choose to reflect upon the answers and open up some of the main points for discussions around the next steps. Usually, you'll find that there are some immediate points that can be added straight to your best practices guide, while with other points, taking action may require next steps internally.

Either way, you'll have a living and breathing document that everyone has contributed to and feels responsible for. I recommend that you follow up and send out the final best practices version to everyone and schedule a 90-day follow-up workshop. It's important to ensure everyone is accountable and that improvements to this guide can be added over time as organizational changes happen.

While I strongly advise you to customize your own team's solution in the creation of meeting best practices, here is a list of general best practices that your team can use and reflect upon.

CHECKLIST FOR MEETING FACILITATORS

Ensure you only invite people who need to be at the meeting and ☐
specify who may be optional. Provide an agenda upfront so you can
invite people for the part of the meeting they are required to attend.

Look at everyone's calendar to ensure you're not creating overlap, ☐
or booking meetings over scheduled lunches, deep work time or
after work hours.

Consider social buffer time before the meeting to chat about ☐
non-work-related topics, especially on a Monday morning.

Consider running meetings for shorter periods of time to keep ☐
engagement high, such as 45 minutes, 25 minutes or even 15 minutes.

If you do have to create a meeting for an hour or longer, ensure ☐
you schedule time for breaks within that meeting.

Attach an agenda to the meeting invite so everyone knows ☐
what to prepare ahead of time and you maximize everyone's time
spent within the meeting.

A highly effective meeting invite should include:

- Details of the time, place and agenda of the meeting. This information should be attached to the meeting invite.
- Details of what is expected of each participant, i.e. particular information or preparation of documents.
- Information as to the specific ASK of each agenda item, i.e. for information, challenge and build, or for decision.
- Any supporting documents or pre-read material.

CHECKLIST FOR MEETING ETIQUETTE

Default to cameras on. Body language accounts for 55 per cent of how we communicate, so without cameras, we can lack effective communication (Mehrabian and Ferris, 1967). ☐

Mute when you're not talking during meetings. ☐

Try not to do other work during meetings. If you're overwhelmed with your workload, consider creating some space for deep work (see diary and calendar management) so that you can be fully present in whatever you're doing. ☐

Asynchronous communication

As I wrote previously, asynchronous communication (async) is when we communicate with each other in a delayed time. It is the process of transmitting information wherein the receiver and sender don't have to be available at the same time. This can be done regardless of the receiver's availability. There is a delay from the time the message is sent to the time the receiver views the message. Some examples of asynchronous communication in remote teams are:

- emails;
- messages sent through instant chat tools like Slack, Teams and messaging tools;

- communication done through project management tools;
- comments, updates and feedback through documents and presentations.

This type of communication is flexible, as opposed to the rigid approach synchronous communication requires, although many teams fall into the trap of believing that async communication needs to be answered immediately and that they have to be always available. For example, I spoke to a professional recently who believed he had to treat his Slack messages from his colleagues like he would a normal conversation in the office – instant responsiveness. This is the fundamental belief we need to change about these tools to help our teams understand that they are built for a delay in responsiveness. Async offers teams a chance to respond when they have time and reap the benefits of not having to attend a meeting in real time in order to collaborate, make decisions and even problem-solve.

While most remote teams are already communicating in a synchronous and asynchronous way, improving async communication offers even more opportunity for your teams to reduce the number of meetings they need. If your teams are spending most of their working weeks in meetings, they are not:

1 being creative and innovative, because they are constantly in a state of reaction to the communication;

2 working in a flexible way that allows them to create space for deep work;

3 getting the opportunity to take quality breaks away from work and live out their self-care practices when working from home.

Simply put, if we are driving the back-to-back meeting culture and NOT leveraging new ways of communicating aside from meetings and emails, we're not empowering our teams with the flexibility that is fundamental for their wellbeing, creativity and mental health. When we work on different schedules and are available at different times, async can become a process that supports diversity in our ways of working and how we want to work.

Asynchronous communication has been around for some time. The very first version of what would become known as email was invented in 1965 at the Massachusetts Institute of Technology, and allowed users to share files and messages on a central disk, logging in from remote terminals. Since then we've come a long way in the development of technologies and, therefore, we have the ability to fully do our jobs and fulfil our work duties from anywhere we can find a WiFi connection. However, even though emails have been around for many years, it doesn't necessarily mean we are all experts at ensuring our emails are efficient, effective and optimized. Many organizations fall into the trap of 'too many emails' and it impacts teams in a negative way. Employees spend too much of their time responding to emails and trying to whittle down their inboxes until they reach zero, only to be met with a full inbox again the next morning. The cycle can seem never-ending. When everyone with an email address has the power to send an email to anyone anytime, without a designated framework or standard procedures, it's very common for emails to suck and drain a large portion of an organization's time.

The benefits of asynchronous communication

Let's look at the benefits of having a clear understanding of and structured process for async communication and how it can help you and your distributed team in a number of ways.

IMPROVE YOUR PRODUCTIVITY

With this communication setup, you can exchange messages no matter what time zone each of your employees is working in. You can open your doors to employees from various parts of the globe without worrying about the time difference. When organizations are able to scale effective async communication, they are able to scale their teams globally.

THE RECIPIENT CAN TAKE SOME TIME TO THINK ABOUT THE RESPONSE.

When an immediate response is required, teams cannot take time to prepare a response that is more elaborate and well thought out. Async gives us a chance to truly reflect, gather interesting points of information and even do some research ahead of sharing our response.

LESS DISTRACTION

Without the need to reply instantly to all messages received, you won't have to worry about getting distracted during meetings. This also allows teams to focus on their work and simply read messages once they have the time. Of course, ineffective asynchronous communication and collaboration can hinder productivity and it's important to establish clear, healthy boundaries and best practices around technology as a team.

The risks of asynchronous communication

Asynchronous communication can also bring a number of challenges to your team, like an overwhelming number of emails and notifications. Here are some ways async can actually hinder the team's productivity in the long term if it's not used correctly.

PROCRASTINATION, AVOIDANCE OR MISSED INFORMATION

Because this setup does not require the recipient to be present during the delivery of the message, they can choose to avoid or prolong the gap between their receipt of the message and sending their response. A good way to get past this issue is by implementing rules about the use of the right communication tools depending on the need or urgency of a message and response. Also, you can use a communication tool that provides the sender with a confirmation of the receipt of the message. On remote teams, a simple acknowledgement by emoji can be an effective way to recognize a message and can be established in a team's best practices guide.

The level of urgency is something that can create confusion amongst remote teams if not clearly defined. If everything is urgent, nothing is urgent, but luckily teams today have the opportunity to leverage project management tools that can support them in setting timelines and timeframes. As leaders, it's important to define what information is urgent and non-urgent for your team and ensure you are clearly setting the expectations. It can be helpful for teams to establish a system for timely interactions with each other through written communication tools like Slack and email. Simply including the timeframe in the message can suffice in helping team members prioritize the tasks they receive throughout the day. Teams can even explore some creative ways to help communicate the level of urgency and timelines. For example, the use of emojis such as coloured circles (red for urgent, orange for important and green for normal) can support the team in visually skimming through emails and messages and helping them understand which message needs their attention first.

ASYNC LACKS GENUINE 'SOCIAL PRESENCE'

Asynchronous communication alone will not be a sufficient way of communicating with your team members if you want to create an engaging and collaborative environment for your team. Recall that 55 per cent of how we communicate is done through our body language, and 35 per cent through tone of voice, meaning if we can't see or hear our colleagues, we are missing out on vital social cues and key elements of communicating together. Even companies that promote asynchronous communication heavily, like Basecamp, discuss how this delayed style of communication isn't suitable for sensitive or difficult topics.

For most teams, the opportunity in async lies in improved use of their current tools, before adding additional technologies to their toolkits.

How to improve asynchronous communication

OPEN AND CLOSED COMMUNICATION LOOP CYCLES

To improve our communication asynchronously and address delays in feedback loops, we have to ask better questions. For example, in an open communication loop cycle, communication goes back and forth several times in order for participants to understand each other and/or make a decision. The purpose of asynchronous communication is to make us more effective and save us time, but when the loop cycle constantly remains open, it defeats that purpose. For example, emailing back and forth for several days isn't an effective way of communicating. In most cases like this, a quick 15-minute conversation on a video call could be all that's needed for both parties to close the communication loop.

Another common example of open-loop communication is through instant messaging tools like Slack. Oftentimes, we don't communicate fully when sending a message, which requires the receiver to ask more questions to determine exactly what's needed and by when. Teams that don't share a standard of how to communicate in tools like Slack fall victim to these loop cycles, and thus turn their internal communication systems into a chaotic, noisy environment, making it difficult to find, read, catch up on and even share information. It can feel somewhat like a virtual battlefield and, as mentioned in a previous chapter, can play havoc with our nervous systems, resulting in stressful environments. When we don't use these tools intentionally with consideration of everyone's time and wellbeing, our remote working environments can turn into a notification minefield.

FIGURE 7.1 Examples of 'under-communication' and 'over-communication'

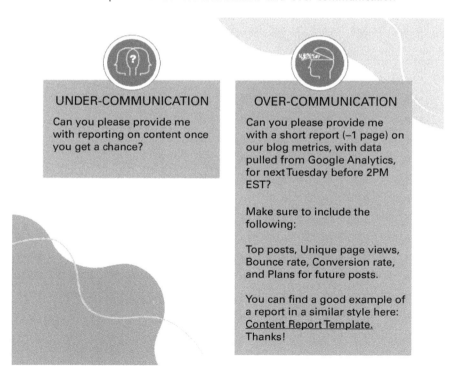

UNDER-COMMUNICATION

Can you please provide me with reporting on content once you get a chance?

OVER-COMMUNICATION

Can you please provide me with a short report (–1 page) on our blog metrics, with data pulled from Google Analytics, for next Tuesday before 2PM EST?

Make sure to include the following:

Top posts, Unique page views, Bounce rate, Conversion rate, and Plans for future posts.

You can find a good example of a report in a similar style here: Content Report Template. Thanks!

ASKING BETTER QUESTIONS

Another key element that can support teams in building more effective async processes is around asking better questions – poorly phrased questions are another way the loop cycle can remain open. Using messaging platforms inefficiently by not clearly articulating our written communication can lead to miscommunication, duplication of efforts and even wasted time.

Consider getting the under-communicated version of this question in your workday (see Figure 7.1). You'd be left confused, with a lot of additional questions. You'd probably waste a lot of time trying to understand exactly what the question means. Instead, if we received a question similar to what's shown under 'over-communication' we would take that task and prioritize it.

If your colleagues are under-communicating, ask them for the following information:

- Information to cover all follow-up questions; overcommunicate.
- A deadline. When do you need a response? How urgent is it? Which task is being blocked right now, pending this action?
- Links, images, and as much supporting material as possible.

Before asking a question, ask yourself the following: *What do I want to get out of this communication? Approval on a task? An asset of some kind?* Written communication should always be extremely clear.

Our objective should be to create calm communication within our teams and in the platforms they use, especially if we want to reduce burnout and create sustainable and productive teams. In the 2017 report 'Stress in America: The State of Our Nation', the American Psychological Association found that US adults who report that they constantly or often check their email, texts and social media accounts were significantly more stressed than those who don't check them as frequently (Doppel, 2017). Creating more calm within our team's communication can allow them to decrease ineffective shallow work and collaboration and prioritize more time towards deeper work and collaboration for themselves and their colleagues.

HOW TO START IMPROVING ASYNCHRONOUS COMMUNICATION

To combat this common issue, I'd recommend running a similar activity to that mentioned above in the synchronous communication section. For organizations that are new to improving their asynchronous processes, I'd suggest first looking at emails and your instant messaging platform.

When you start to see the results and positive impacts of having shared team best practices around synchronous and asynchronous communication, I invite you to leverage my resources guide online at www.operateremote.com/book, which will support you in introducing new tools specifically for your remote organization.

Reflect upon the current synchronous processes that are causing friction within your team or maybe just aren't working anymore. In the case of one of my clients, it was a daily morning standup for their developer team. The standup had been established for over a year. It served a great purpose – information sharing and an opportunity for the team to see each other on video calls, connect and set themselves up for the day. However, more recently, since the team had grown in number, the standup wasn't as effective. In fact, the meeting, which used to take 15 minutes, was now sometimes extending to 40 minutes. It wasn't the best use of everyone's time but the team still wanted the opportunity to connect each morning – it was important to them as remote workers.

On an organizational level, it cost the company a lot of money – in spite of growing numbers, the whole development team was 'offline' for 40 minutes every morning. In addition, some of the team members wanted to do deep work at that time in the morning, when they felt most productive. Some team members mentioned that they weren't really morning people and wanted to take more advantage of the company's flexible work policy. When I delivered training to the team, this issue was brought up. The opportunity for change presented in the form of leveraging asynchronous communication.

We decided to move the 'information sharing' piece of their standup to asynchronous communication using Microsoft Teams, which allowed the daily standup check-in questions to be sent out to all team members asynchronously in their Teams channel. They had a certain allocated time to complete the question fields and once they did, everyone else on their team could see their answers. One of the questions they asked was, 'What would you like to problem solve or share in our team standup and how will it benefit everyone on the team?' The answers that came back were around different challenges or problems team members faced and even new learnings that could benefit everyone else. The team would then choose, together, the most important blockers. They still used their original 15-minute daily standup time, but moved the meeting to later in the morning. This time was then spent problem solving together as a team and focused on deep collaboration. The team still had their quality time together and check-in every day, but the new process was much more effective and the communication of much higher quality. This type of conversation stimulated the right part of their brain – their creativity. It promoted an environment of active participation which led to higher engagement, and why wouldn't it? It's exciting to brainstorm and problem-solve amongst a team of smart colleagues.

This resulted in the team not only reclaiming more time in their mornings but also becoming much more engaged. The meeting format changed, with a focus on coming together as a team to brainstorm and problem solve, and thus their appetite for winning as a team increased.

Asynchronous communication will be indispensable. It is just as essential as its counterpart and, by implementing the right rules and methods, async can help you improve your team's productivity, communication and camaraderie.

Below are some guidelines that you can use as conversation starters with your team on how they can improve their asynchronous communication using instant messaging tools like Slack and direct emails. These are only examples, and some may or may not be applicable to your team. Please use these guidelines as an idea generator and a way to bring your team together to create their own best practices for asynchronous communication.

THE DOS AND DON'TS OF USING MESSAGING TOOLS

Do

Set your messaging tools status to active and include your working hours so others know when you are available to ensure work visibility. ☐

Use 'Do Not Disturb' according to your work schedule or when you need to focus. Please respect this status when others use it, as the person may not answer right away. ☐

Re-read your message to ensure the tone of your language will land with the receiver correctly. ☐

Have fun – we don't have the benefit of being able to 'chat' in a conventional way at work, so use messaging tools to connect with your teammates! ☐

Let the receiver(s) know the level of urgency required for your question. This will help everyone manage their time and workloads better. ☐

Don't

Don't send one message as multiple pings. Include your question or note in one paragraph and send it as one full message. This ensures we don't disturb people too much. ☐

Don't have group discussions on processes/ideas that require follow-up actions on a message platform. If a process or idea needs to be discussed, ensure that a meeting is scheduled and actions are recorded. This ensures nothing is lost amongst the chain of messages. ☐

Don't try to handle constructive feedback in an email or message. If constructive feedback requires a bit more explanation, it's best to do this on a video call/meeting to ensure mutual understanding and reduce the opportunity for miscommunication. If you're operating in a hybrid team, move these conversations to in-person meetings. ☐

Don't send direct messages late at night and be mindful of the different time zones in the group chats – please respect others' time off work. Try using messaging tools workflow to send messages at a set time. ☐

BEST PRACTICES FOR USING EMAIL

Before sending an email, consider:

- Would a phone call be more appropriate or have more impact?
    - Are you hiding behind an impersonal email?
    - Make sure that everyone you are emailing actually needs to be included.
    - Emails should only be sent 'To' those who are expected to take action.
    - Please do not 'CC' unless necessary as this can impact productivity. Use the 'CC' line for people who simply need your information (FYI) updates.
- Never reply 'All' when thanking or acknowledging someone over email. Only reply to that person or someone you specifically want to be aware of the action.
- Email should be used to confirm decisions that have been made.
- Try to avoid 'conversations' over email that could be handled better in a meeting.
- Ensure the subject line of the email is specific and searchable.
- Use the 'too long don't read' (TLDR) functionality at the beginning of an email that's more than two paragraphs long. Here you should include a summary of your email to make it easier for colleagues to skim through.
- Before sending an email give some thought to the style of your message.
- Be mindful of punctuation and language.
- Try to imagine receiving the email from yourself – how would you FEEL/ react? Communications can affect someone's emotional wellbeing for the whole day.
- Be concise and to the point while being respectful, answering all questions and attempting to pre-empt further questions.
- Utilize shared drives and folders and provide the relevant link/ instructions in the email.
- If you have to email at the weekend (which shouldn't be the norm), schedule your emails to be sent on Monday morning instead of sending them to colleagues over the weekend.

CASE STUDY
Communication and performance management

A client of mine approached me when they were transitioning into a remote environment, having previously created and grown a team primarily in an office setting. It was 2020, and while the opportunity offered by remote working was significant, they had never worked in this way before and had some concerns. The main objective was to create a world-class employee experience in a remote and virtual environment and we did just that. My goal was to bring out the amazing characteristics that this team already possessed, but to do so in a way that was optimized for remote environments.

Communication wasn't optimized for remote environments

Like the majority of teams that transition to remote working overnight, this company found challenges with the team's internal communication. They had previously relied on office-based communication, working together in person in one office location every day.

Moving to a remote working environment, it was clear how much the team relied on synchronous communication and how much time it consumed in everyone's day. This led to an increase in meetings and interruptions, which impacted the team's ability to focus on work – which was fundamental in the team's ability to innovate and strategize. We worked together to develop the team's understanding of both synchronous and asynchronous communication in remote environments. In a way similar to the examples above, we worked together to develop a list of synchronous and asynchronous best practices that empowered the team to improve their team communication so that they could:

- reduce the number of poor-quality meetings and have more effective ones;
- create more space and time in their calendars for innovation and deep work;
- leverage settings and functionalities of their tools like Slack to make communication more efficient;
- avoid feeling overwhelmed by emails, notifications or meetings;
- feel up to date with what they needed to know;
- reduce open communication loops to save everyone time.

We created this initiative in collaboration with the team, which resulted in this project's success. The team witnessed the benefits and ROI from working on their communication, and how it makes it easier to hold themselves and each other accountable in remote environments.

We rolled out a 'Spring Clean Communication Guide' (download it at www.operateremote.com/book). As a remote-first company, how the team communicates is fundamental to their effectiveness as individuals and as a team. This guide empowered everyone to step back and assess the effectiveness of their communication.

It's easy to fall into a trap where we don't question meetings, but accept them without thinking. However, at some point, we realize that the value of these meetings has been diluted, resulting in our time being wasted. Every spring, the team will continue to implement a company-wide Spring Communication Clean to ensure that everyone:

- has meaningful meetings that are of value;
- has enough time and flexibility in their day to do deep work;
- is communicating in the most effective ways possible;
- isn't wasting time being in meetings that are not important.

From surveying the team after the communication project, it was clear that the work we did together paid off. About 74 per cent of the team strongly agreed that in a remote work setting they know what is expected of them and 90 per cent of the team stated they were confident and happy about the transition to remote working.

The shift from input to output in performance

The team also needed a scalable process for performance management. Our objective was to align managers and employees on how performance reviews would be conducted for specific roles. We needed to create a process that embodied the culture of the team and a performance management structure that compensated for performance on an individual and a team level, while also empowering the team to create their own goals and objectives.

Unlike other organizations that have one annual performance review, they wanted a process for ongoing feedback, which they felt was fundamental in optimizing performance as a team and as individuals. At a company level, they were constantly seeking new ways to advance and improve their products, technology and vision.

On a cultural level, they wanted to create an environment that empowered their team to become the best versions of themselves. To do great things, they knew they needed to be a collection of people who all operate at their personal best. It was about having a growth mindset and the understanding that where you are today has no relevance to where you can be tomorrow.

We collected data in several ways from hiring managers and individual contributors as to what they'd like to see in a newly revised review process. It was clear that we needed a process that would last for the long term. The team had previously tried to implement several performance-based processes, but always seemed to come up against challenges. Our main objective was to create a performance process that was fair and clear, and gave team members autonomy. To do so, we created a performance management structure that focused on the output of work that empowered the team to:

- set their own specific, measurable, attainable, relevant and time-bound (SMART) goals – both personally and professionally, based on the company's key yearly objectives;
- have transparency on their incentivization based on their level of goal achievement;
- feel supported throughout the goal-setting process through goal-setting training and leadership support.

Our newly formed process ensured that all hiring managers had:

- a process and understanding of how to support their team in creating meaningful SMART goals;
- a checklist for consistent goal-based conversations;
- transparency on what incentives they can or cannot provide to their team.

The success of this project was overwhelmingly positive. Leaders stated that engagement increased and their teams were more responsible as a result of being able to set their own goals and understand how they were being measured as employees. In fact, our final survey resulted in 74 per cent of the team strongly agreeing that they understood how their performance was being measured at an individual and company level. This is the benefit of providing clarity on performance and expectations – when everyone is clear, everyone can thrive.

Remote-first processes require continuous effort and improvement. While there are many areas of process improvement for your organization to cover, I always suggest starting with the area that is consuming the most of your teams' time – in my experience, it's usually meetings. Starting with the process that is the biggest time drainer will free up more time for everyone within the organization and lead to higher engagement that creates a bandwidth for more opportunities to develop and improve even more team processes.

References

Anderson, A H, McEwan, R, Bal, J and Carletta, J (2007) Virtual team meetings: An analysis of communication and context, *Computers in Human Behavior*, 23 (5), pp 2558–80, www.sciencedirect.com/science/article/abs/pii/S0747563207000027 (archived at https://perma.cc/F64J-PQJB)

Basecamp (2022) Work from home, the Basecamp way, https://basecamp.com/remote-resources (archived at https://perma.cc/WDF6-LF7J)

Brake, T (2006) Leading global virtual teams, *Industrial and Commercial Training*, 1 April, www.emerald.com/insight/content/doi/10.1108/00197850610659364/full/html (archived at https://perma.cc/3577-P63R)

Doppel (2017) American Psychological Association finds higher levels of stress in constant phone checkers, *Doppel*, 4 October, https://feeldoppel.com/blogs/news/american-psychological-association-finds-higher-levels-of-stress-in-constant-phone-checkers (archived at https://perma.cc/3BWF-JRHJ)

Dow, W and Taylor, B (2008) *Project Management Communications Bible*, Wiley Publishing Inc., Indianapolis, Indiana

Duarte, D L and Snyder, N T (2000) *Mastering Virtual Teams: Strategies, Tools, and Techniques that Succeed,* 2nd edn, Jossey-Bass, San Francisco

GitLab (nd) GitLab's guide to all-remote, https://about.gitlab.com/company/culture/all-remote/guide (archived at https://perma.cc/JU87-L3FK)

Gourani, S (2021) Why most meetings fail before they even begin, *Forbes*, 6 May, www.forbes.com/sites/soulaimagourani/2021/05/06/why-most-meetings-fail-before-they-even-begin (archived at https://perma.cc/7Z2B-AVLL)

Griffis, H (2018) Everything we know about remote work, *Buffer Blog*, 27 August, https://buffer.com/resources/remote-work (archived at https://perma.cc/6ZGU-M8EK)

Keyzerman, Y. (2003) Trust in virtual teams, IEEE Xplore, https://ieeexplore.ieee.org/document/1245520 (archived at https://perma.cc/U9T7-FV6A)

Lee-Kelley, L, Crossman, A and Cannings, A (2004) A social interaction approach to managing the 'invisibles' of virtual teams, *Industrial Management & Data Systems*, 104 (8), pp 650–7, https://doi.org/10.1108/02635570410561636 (archived at https://perma.cc/8NZY-3GCX)

Lerner, S M (2008) Leadership best practices that enhance the perceived effectiveness of global distributed hybrid teams, *ProQuest*, www.proquest.com/openview/af8342ac67e9a76d0cf5b4b396fc6d34/1 (archived at https://perma.cc/QL6G-M46V)

Mehrabian, A and Ferris, S R (1967) Inference of attitudes from nonverbal communication in two channels, *Journal of Consulting Psychology*, 31 (3), pp 248–252, https://psycnet.apa.org/doiLanding?doi=10.1037%2Fh0024648 (archived at https://perma.cc/UA75-U5XE)

Moran, S (2021) Reducing proximity bias on your remote team, *Operate Remote Newsletter*, 30 November, www.linkedin.com/pulse/reducing-proximity-bias-your-remote-team-shauna-moran (archived at https://perma.cc/WY2Y-9SJT)

Oertig, M and Buergi, T (2006) The challenges of managing cross-cultural virtual project teams, *Team Performance Management*, 12 (1/2), pp 23–30, https://doi.org/10.1108/13527590610652774 (archived at https://perma.cc/F8DB-VSY5)

Plazas, P (2013) Challenges of managing a virtual team with an ocean in between, *PM World Journal*, https://pmworldlibrary.net/wp-content/uploads/2013/02/PMWJ6-Jan2013-PLAZAS-Challenges-of-Managing-Virtual-Team-UTD-SecondEdition.pdf (archived at https://perma.cc/3Y4K-MQHV)

Virtira (2021) Exhausted or engaged? Meeting on camera during the pandemic, https://info.virtira.com/webcam-survey (archived at https://perma.cc/965B-9THP)

Vohra, R (2021) The state of your inbox in 2021: email burnout and browsing in bed, *Superhuman*, 21 April, https://blog.superhuman.com/the-state-of-your-inbox-in-2021 (archived at https://perma.cc/Z6AH-WHLJ)

The Organization: summary

In section two, The Organization, we covered the main root causes on an organizational level as to why individuals experience burnout in their working environments. We also looked at the cultural impacts of burnout on the right to disconnect and purpose, and the true cost of burnt-out teams on organizations. In the final chapter of this section we covered the main ways organizations can support their teams in reducing burnout and overwhelm through the creation of remote-first processes. Below is a summary of the key reflection points that you can leverage for conversations within your own team.

Measuring the impact of burnout

Here are some metrics that organizations can collect to better under-stand the impact that burnout is having on their bottom line:

- How many hours of work are missed by employees for absenteeism and stress leave.
- Time spent on coaching and supporting employees with stress or performance issues that stemmed from burnout at work (by both HR departments and all levels of management).
- Turnover rates in your organization and the costs associated with replacing departing employees.
- Project errors, misplaced timelines or unmet deadlines.

Reduce unfair treatment at work

- Have clear, up-to-date policies.
- Assess leaders based on feedback from team members on their experiences with their direct manager.
- Educate leaders on what unfair treatment looks like in the workplace so they can better identify other leaders who aren't following fair procedures and behaviours.

Creating equality in a hybrid workplace

Leaders who manage both remote and office-based team members should review their activities to ensure that they are connecting with team members regardless of where they are working from on a regular basis. Here are some questions that leaders can start to ask themselves:

- Have I connected with remote and office-based team members equally this week?
- How have I created a level playing field for remote and office-based team members to communicate and collaborate?
- How have I checked in with remote team members to ensure they feel included in office-based activities?

Creating supportive leaders

Here are strategies that organizations can use to help their leaders to better support their team members:

- Limit the number of direct reports each leader has.
- Reduce workloads for leaders by understanding that the majority of their workload and responsibilities should be taken up with supporting and coaching team members to their greatest potential.
- Develop team leaders' skills around emotional intelligence, active listening and coaching.

Creating realistic timelines

Here are some ways that leaders can support their teams in creating realistic timeframes and due dates for their workloads:

- Reality-test delegated timelines by asking relevant questions around how each team member envisions fulfilling this work, such as:
  - How do you see yourself completing this task with this timeline in conjunction with your other tasks and priorities?

○ How realistic does this seem to you right now?

○ What might need to be put on hold or reprioritized for now?

○ By taking on this work, will your healthy workday habits be impacted? If so, how?

○ How will you ensure you're not overworking to get this done? What could be delegated away from you right now that can help?

Remote-first processes: synchronous communication

ONE-ON-ONE MEETINGS

Review your one-on-one recurring meetings and ask yourself:

• Do you need to have this meeting? What's the value of this meeting for both parties?

• Can the cadence of this meeting be changed? For example, once a month, every two weeks, every six weeks?

• Can the duration of this meeting be changed? For example, 45 minutes instead of 60?

• Is this meeting at a convenient time for me and the other participants?

TEAM MEETINGS

Review your team's recurring meetings and ask yourself:

• What's the value of this meeting? Are we aligned as a group on the purpose and value of this meeting, or do we need to revisit this together?

• How is this discussion contributing to our goal?

• What's the desired outcome?

• Does this meeting have an agenda each week? If not, who should take responsibility for this agenda?

• Does this meeting have a set of action items each week that includes a clear ask from all participants?

- Do I need to be at this meeting or is there someone else at my department who is attending and can fill me in afterwards?

- Do we clearly summarize the discussion of the meeting and take notes on the next steps to inform the next agenda? If not, who can take responsibility for that?

- Can we reduce the length of time we spend in this meeting? What would make sense?

- How about the cadence? Do we need to have this meeting as often as we do?

Remote-first processes: asynchronous communication

Here are some important elements of asynchronous communication that you can further explore within your team and organization:

- Open and closed communication cycles – asking questions.
- Create a list of best practices for messaging tools, e.g. Slack.
- Create a list of best practices for using emails.

Remote-first processes: performance management

Here are some important elements of asynchronous communication that you can further explore within your team and organization. Review performance management focuses on a shift from input to output:

- Identify each team's capacity.
- Break down individual workloads.
- Continuously seek to discover bandwidth.

PART THREE

The Leader

8

The differences between leading remote and office-based teams

In the first part of the book, we looked at the individual – how we, as unique human beings, can reduce burnout based on our perceptions, beliefs and ways of working. We looked at the core elements of emotional intelligence that can support us in reducing stress in how we work remotely. When looking at the root causes of burnout in remote teams, it's also essential that we seek to understand how organizations and culture can contribute to employee wellness and resilience.

Leadership accounts for up to 70 per cent of employee engagement, meaning leaders' opportunity to influence their remote teams is enormous. But how can we effectively support leaders in developing the right skills, specifically for managing people in a virtual environment (Beck and Harter, 2015)? How do we equip leaders with the right tools, information and guidance to mitigate burnout and stress in their remote team members? Before we explore these essential skills and attributes needed for successfully managing remote teams, let's take a look at the main differences in managing office teams versus remote teams.

Lack of water cooler moments

When you work at the office, at the water cooler you're likely to hear passing conversations about what is going on in the lives of your team members. Maybe you've heard that their newborn baby isn't sleeping well and, as a result, it's been a challenge for them to get up in the mornings. Or possibly you realized that you and another colleague share a passion for the same sports team or hike trails. Regardless of what these conversations are about, they are part of the foundation in building relationships and getting to know our team members.

However, remote working can feel very transactional without these natural flows of casual conversations. Working virtually means we often have to be proactive in spending time building relationships and it's often the first thing to fall off our to-do list when we're busy. Leaders in virtual environments today need to go above and beyond to facilitate these interactions with each of their team members and help them connect on this level. It's within these conversations that we can get to really know a person beyond their working style or professional achievements. With that understanding, we can better build empathy towards our colleagues by finding common ground and interests outside of just working together as a team.

Issues can go unnoticed

A lack of casual conversations, not seeing people in person and not being able to check in with a person outside of their job responsibilities can lead to issues going unnoticed. In the chapter 'What is Burnout?' we uncovered some of the major red flags that can help leaders to identify if a team member is feeling overwhelmed. It's important for leaders to familiarize themselves with these red flags, and to reflect on past experiences from which they can learn.

To give you an example, a couple of years ago a client of mine was concerned about his team members. As a leader of a remote team he always prioritized building relationships with his team and having open dialogue. With one particular team member he had recently noticed a dip in performance, which was very unusual. After a couple of days, he started to become increasingly concerned. We worked together on creating a framework so that he could address the performance issues but still lead with empathy and openness regarding the reasons for poor performance. What this leader found out blew him away. Although this team member had worked closely with him for years, he found it difficult to be open as to what was really going on. A close family member had been diagnosed with a life-threatening illness and, understandably, he had been struggling to focus on work. How relieved that leader was that he approached that conversation with care and empathy. I often think about how this situation might have played out if this team worked together in person. There probably would have been a lot more opportunities to disclose this very difficult news. While we should never just 'accept' underperformance issues, as leaders we need to approach each situation by recognizing that we know absolutely nothing about what is going on in that person's life. We must lead with positive intent in all situations and understand that there is much more going on in the life of the human, behind the screen, than we could possibly imagine. These are the leaders we need to reduce burnout on our remote teams.

Social cues can be missed

When we're working together in person, in an office, it's easier for leaders to connect socially with their team members. Water cooler moments, coffee chats and hallway acknowledgements are normal everyday occurrences. Leaders can physically see if a team member's mood has changed, their body language has shifted or their face shows confusion or anxiety. It's often easier, on site, for a team member to approach their leader or find time to chat in a less formal way if an issue arises. Working and communicating together in person every day can more easily allow for issues to be mitigated before they become a huge problem. In contrast, if an issue arises when working remotely, a colleague may be more likely to wait until the 'right' time to discuss the issue with their leader, or even wait until they have a formal check-in meeting. And if leaders aren't having regular one-on-one conversations with their team, you can see how the problem might escalate. I call this the 'remote rabbit hole'.

The remote rabbit hole

A remote rabbit hole is a situation where we misunderstand communication and take a comment personally by misinterpreting a message, whether it's a verbal comment, written note, or even a facial expression. It's a common issue and not only have I seen it myself many times, I have coached remote workers on it many times. Misreading and misinterpreting communication is even more common remotely, because if the opportunity to extinguish the issue or perception isn't offered close to the event itself, the chance of the issue being internalized is greater. The more it is internalized, the bigger the challenge can seem. The remote rabbit hole doesn't just impact individual contributors, it can affect all employees within an organization, regardless of the position or level they hold.

I recently worked with a client who was a relatively new director in his organization. At a leadership meeting the CEO had made a comment about how they needed to ensure they didn't make mistakes as they had before when hiring senior leadership. This new director took this comment to heart and went down the remote rabbit hole:

- Does that mean that the CEO thinks I was a wrong hire?

- Does that mean that I am not good enough at my job?

- Does that mean I'm not performing to the right standards?

Having worked directly with the CEO myself, I knew how excited the CEO was about this director and his ability to make change within the organization. I knew that this comment was made as a generalization, not personally against this director.

However, as a coach, I needed the director to see this for himself. 'What evidence do you have to support that this comment was personalized against you?' I asked. 'Well, I don't have any evidence really. There is nothing tangible that would suggest I'm a bad hire. It's just this comment,' he replied. 'Okay, so let's do a reality test. What evidence do you have that this comment *wasn't* about you?' I probed. 'Well, I met with the CEO last week, and he said he's happy with my department's performance and goals for this quarter. He said he was happy to have me on the team and he's excited for the year ahead,' he said.

'That's great,' I said. 'Sounds like you have a lot of evidence that would suggest you have nothing to worry about. But let's look at the comment that was made, and try to think through some of the context. Think about the hiring decisions that were made in the past. What's up with the hiring process right now?' I asked. 'Yeah,' he replied. 'We made some mistakes last year with two leaders in particular and we've all discussed before how we're improving our interviewing and qualifying process to ensure it doesn't happen again.' 'Okay, so it sounds like you have more evidence to support the fact that this comment was just made as a generalization. What are your thoughts on this now?' I probed. He replied, 'I now know that the way I internalized that comment isn't true. I sat on this all weekend – wondering, worrying and convincing myself of a story that I totally made up in my head!'

This leader had identified his limiting perception of the situation and realized that he had built this up in his head without reality-testing the situation or what was said. He went down the remote rabbit hole. Thankfully, this leader had access to a coach, like me, who could help him 'catch' this before it became a huge problem. He did mention that he was considering looking for other job opportunities because he had believed so deeply that the comment was about him and he was a bad hire for the organization. He was a great leader, and cared so deeply about his performance as a high-achieving professional that he needed feedback to grow and to be reassured. In addition, when we start a new job or project, 'imposter syndrome' and self-doubt can creep in. Further, this leader did mention he was feeling more stressed out than usual.

If this situation had happened in an office environment, what do you think would have happened? This director would have probably met the CEO in the hallway or in the office kitchen and had a casual conversation. He either would have sussed the situation out by checking in on the CEO's reaction to him in general, or brought up the comment about the wrong hiring decision and had a chance to understand exactly what the CEO meant.

In summary, when we work in person we have access to data that we don't remotely. By data I mean we can interpret someone's facial expressions and body language and understand what's being said behind the words. If this comment had been made at an in-person meeting, normally we'd feel much more comfortable and able to interrupt and ask for clarity on the comment in the moment. We have more opportunities to connect with people over coffee or tea or even in the hallway, so we can reality-test our interpretations.

Preventing the remote rabbit hole

So how do we prevent ourselves and our team members from going down the remote rabbit hole when we work remotely and don't have the opportunity to reality-test in person? We start by creating and nurturing psychological safety within our teams. Psychological safety is the ability for employees to feel safe when speaking up, giving feedback or doing a particular task. In the case of speaking up, feeling psychologically safe means team members feel comfortable and supported in being able to ask questions, reality-test assumptions and ask for alternative viewpoints. Teams with a higher level of psychological safety are often the teams that have established how they can build trust within their organizations and amongst their team members. To create this level of psychological safety within remote teams, leaders not only need to create dedicated time for discussion around potential issues or challenges, but they also need to build high levels of trust with each individual on their team.

Building trust and psychological safety

Trust is a fundamental aspect of any business. It's also the lifeline of successful remote and hybrid (office and remote) teams. As human beings, we tend to give our trust to people we have physically met in person. There are many reasons for this, such as body language, eye contact, spending more time together socially and meeting people in person every day (Ferrell and Kline, 2018).

So, how is it possible to build a trusting relationship between our workforce and our teams, whether you are working remotely or at the office? Leaders can build trust through communication, but it requires a proactive approach and an awareness of how they communicate with their colleagues.

Trust is an aspect of leadership that we often overlook. We can't quantify it, but it accelerates growth in all that we do, both in business and in our personal lives. Trust creates credibility and credibility creates trust. Trust is the lifeline of successful teams and up until the shift to virtual teams, many leaders might have said that they built trust with their teams by seeing them every day in the office and building in-person relationships over time. Most of our trust-building is created by spending time in person with our colleagues and our team. It's created over time when we launch successful projects and confide in one another, getting to know each other on a deeper level. However, we also need to build trust fast in remote teams, so our teams can have psychological safety and ability to speak up, give feedback and share their personal situations and challenges. To do this, leaders are required to seek ways of building trust through a computer screen.

Remote teams have been found to experience trust issues or challenges with trust building, typically when new employees are hired, or employees first work on a project together. Trust issues can also be magnified in remote teams, as lack of personal face-to-face dialogue makes it difficult for personal relationships to be fostered. Several research papers have shown that people build trust more easily with those they meet in person, as opposed to trying to create trusting relationships electronically or virtually (Lee-Kelley et al, 2004). Trust is something that needs consideration at all stages of a team coming together. Crossman and Lee-Kelley (2004) explain that the building of interpersonal and intra-organizational trust and commitment is an important component in the 'storming and norming' stages of the team's development, and without the establishment of mutual trust, reciprocal commitment will not be achieved.

How to build trust in remote teams

So, what can virtual leaders do to not only build trust amongst their team but also fast-track trust in remote environments? The first and most overlooked aspect of trust-building for leaders has to do with mindset and our perception of how trust is built. I often see leaders or people managers with a perception that trust is built upon in-person connections and office performance visibility. It's important, as a leader, to first understand how to define trust for yourself and your colleagues, and to identify what's important to you when it comes to building trusting relationships at work. Often in remote teams, we hire new team members and require them to get up to speed on projects and work responsibilities as soon as possible, especially in fast-paced environments. To do this effectively, it's helpful to think of trust like a battery, similar to the one in your phone.

> When an organization hires employees remotely, that battery must be at least 50 per cent full. Your hiring and interview process should reflect that 50 per cent by being tailored to remote environments. When a new employee joins the team, the trust battery expectations should be explained. As a leader, it's important to reflect upon how the other 50 per cent will be attained. Often that extra 50 per cent of the battery includes things like:
>
> * living into company values and/or behaviours;
> * completing tasks and responsibilities to a certain standard;
> * following through on promises made;
> * sharing insights and personal experiences.

Just as leaders have personal preferences when it comes to how they create and give trust to their team members, employees build trust in their leaders and managers in their own unique ways. Some of the most common ways leaders can help their employees confide and trust in them are:

* following through on promises made;
* giving them dedicated time to be heard and supported in a one-on-one setting – doing this consistently, over time, helps charge up the trust battery;

- sharing personal experiences to help build the 'human side' of the relationship;
- taking time to understand employees' values, motivations and recognition preferences;
- actively listening and being 100 per cent present in employee conversations.

As a remote leader, you must understand that you have to go the extra mile in terms of proactive communication and acknowledgement, and that engaging with your team members will enable you to be successful at building trusting and long-lasting relationships. Here are some questions that can support you in reflecting on the unique ways you build trust as a leader:

- How do I actively listen?
- What powerful questions can I ask my team to build more trust?
- How can I set better expectations for my team?
- How and where can delegation support my team members? How might I use it?
- Where might mutual accountability be important for my team?

How leaders can create psychological safety

The purpose of psychological safety is to create a safe environment in which team members feel comfortable speaking up. Think about psychological safety outside of a work environment, maybe with a partner. If you can freely express how you feel, what's worrying or challenging you, and your ideas for improvement in the relationship, that comes from feeling safe in being able to do so. Most of us don't realize its importance until psychological safety isn't there anymore.

Psychological safety is similar to, but not the same as, trust. Trust generally happens and is built between two people, while psychological safety represents the trust experienced on a team and individual level. For example, it's important that team members can feel safe to speak up in their one-on-one conversations with their leaders, but it's equally as important that they feel safe to speak up in a team setting. Everyone contributes to building a safe environment, not just leaders.

We want to create psychological safety within remote teams, especially when it comes to reducing stress and burnout. We know that to be able to effectively manage burnout on teams, we need to know when there is a problem. We can't address root causes and coach team members to their very best potential if we don't know something is wrong. Our teams won't tell us that something is wrong if they don't feel safe enough to do so.

As leaders, it's important to remember that psychological safety grows and develops over time. There isn't any one action or strategy that you can implement immediately that will increase this safety amongst your team. In fact, it's small everyday actions and behaviours that, over time, lead to teams feeling safe to be 100 per cent themselves in a team setting.

How do we create psychologically safe team environments remotely?

- **Level the meeting participation field:** It's common in remote team meetings for louder personalities to take over or even hijack a meeting and its discussions. It's important for leaders to facilitate meetings effectively so that everyone has equal time to engage, share feedback and speak up about their ideas. Leaders need to create structure around team discussions and kindly redirect conversations or team members that take up too much time. In a remote environment, it can also be beneficial to provide ways outside of just speaking for more quiet or shy team members. For example, using the chat functionality can be a great way to hear feedback on a particular topic, and it makes sure that everyone has equal opportunity for participation. Another great trick I share with managers is to use images as a way to engage more introverted personalities on their remote teams. For example, instead of asking the team, 'How is everyone doing?' you might decide to ask the team to describe how they are doing today using an image. They can then find an image or a GIF and post it in the chat window. As a leader, this provides you with a genuine pulse as to energy and wellbeing, which will allow you to follow up afterwards should you have any concerns. You're also guaranteed some laughs amongst the team!

- **Promote active listening:** Contracting at the start of the meeting is a way to set the tone and best practices for your and your team's time together. For example, you might set the expectation that everyone is present for the next 30 minutes and to do that, turn off any notifications or tabs outside of this meeting. As a leader, it can be beneficial to highlight and explain to your team the benefits of doing this and how active listening can support everyone in feeling heard.

- **Make it easy to ask anything:** It's not enough these days to just state, 'let me know if you have any questions'. This statement is a closed phrase rather than open. An open statement would be, 'What questions do you have right now?' As leaders, embracing the silence and waiting is an important part of the process. Silence promotes speaking up and gives everyone a chance to think about what they want to say.

- **Address individual working styles:** Not everyone works the same and not everyone has the same personality. As a leader your job is to embrace and welcome the fact that not everyone is like you and may work differently than you do. When leaders can start to recognize this diversity, they begin to create diversity in communication and the way the team works. Naturally, team members will start to shift the way they recognize each other's differences. In a remote environment, we need to be proactive around understanding how each other works. For example, do you understand each other's communication preferences? Does someone on your team prefer to communicate in a direct text-based way while others prefer to have more social interaction on a call before getting into work-based projects? It's the little areas of understanding that support team members in feeling understood and therefore being more comfortable in being themselves.

Everyone has different assumptions about what things 'should' look like. If you don't discuss them and you are working in a team, those assumptions will overshadow you in a negative way. Here are some questions to support your team members in deeply understanding each other's unique working styles and preferences. In my experience, having this level of transparency and understanding helps promote and create trust within our teams.

- What would the dream/success look like for us working together?
- What would the nightmare/worst case scenario look like?
- What's the best way for us to work together to achieve success?
- What do we need to be mindful of so we avoid the worst case?
- What permissions do each of us want from each other?
- What will we do when things get hard?

TEAM DISCUSSION AROUND PSYCHOLOGICAL SAFETY

The questions below can support you and your team in establishing what psychological safety looks like to each of you and how it can support you in your work together as a team.

- What comes to mind when you hear the words *psychological safety*?
- What behaviours do you see in our team that reflect psychological safety? How are these expressed remotely?
- What behaviours may signal that psychological safety is lacking in our team?
- Do you feel that psychological safety is important? What difference does it make in a team, and what have you seen on other teams you've worked with?
- What are your takeaways from this conversation?

Trust and burnout summary

In summary, to support our teams in reducing burnout and feeling their very best in the remote workplace, leaders have to focus on building and maintaining truthful relationships. Trusting relationships will help remote team members feel psychologically safe and supported in bringing forth issues or challenges that are getting in the way of them doing their very best work. A trusting relationship also allows for leaders to approach their team members with any concerns or issues with a mutual understanding that these conversations are coming from a place of positive intent – the intent of helping and supporting one another and the wider team to become their very best and live to their highest potential. To build trust remotely, open conversations need to happen, along with personal reflections as to everyone's unique definition of trust. Trust is built through not only the performance or results achieved but also the characteristics, actions and behaviours of the individual on an everyday basis.

So much of this safety within our teams comes from their experiences with how challenges are managed amongst the team. For example, take a team that had a meeting around an error that happened on an important project. Instead of the meeting being focused on learning, opportunities and what to do better next time, the meeting shifted to a black or white view – who did it right and who did it wrong. It easily turned into a blame and shame discussion, often subconsciously. Now, think about the next time any one of those team members makes an error, identifies a potential risk or wants to address a challenge amongst the team – will they feel comfortable in doing so? Probably not. The blame and shame experience is imprinted within their minds and will likely prevent them from sharing what needs to be addressed. It all comes down to having a growth mindset.

Growth and fixed mindset

When it comes to creating safe and trusting environments, there are two major mindsets that prevail in a team's culture (Dweck, 2007):

- **The fixed mindset:** believes that our abilities are fixed and innate. Sees failures as a reflection of our own abilities and skills. Doesn't like to be challenged. Resistance to change as 'this is the way I've always done it' mentality creeps in.

- **The growth mindset:** believes that our skills and abilities can be developed, always. Views failures as opportunities to learn and grow. Sees change as an opportunity to grow as an individual. Seeks out constructive feedback to continually improve.

It can be helpful for leaders to discuss the differences in these mindsets amongst the team themselves to have them consider where they as individuals and as a collective might be limited in their mindset approach. For example, a growth mindset is a belief that people, including oneself, can change their talents, abilities and intelligence. Conversely, those with a fixed mindset do not believe that people can change these things.

Decades of research have found that those with a growth mindset are more mentally primed to approach and take on challenges, take advantage of feedback, adopt the most effective problem-solving strategies, provide developmental feedback to subordinates, and be effortful and persistent in seeking to accomplish goals (Dweck, 2007). Not only that, but when leaders can promote a growth mindset amongst their team members, they give them the support and belief that, over time, their skills and abilities can be developed. What an incredible approach to live by as a leader – to truly believe in the potential of every individual.

In a team setting, it can be helpful to create a common language for team members to easily identify when they might fall into the trap of a fixed mindset, such as blaming or feeling like giving up. Here are some examples that can support you in bringing these conversations to life for your team so that it becomes a deeper part of your culture:

- Growth mindset is more than just being open and flexible; it is also about a dedication to personal development and growth. How are we dedicating ourselves to our own personal growth and to each other's growth?

- Growth mindset is about more than only effort; it is also about process, strategies, focus, perseverance and getting feedback. How can we be more open to celebrating these important attributes as a remote team? How do we recognize feedback as an important element of our success?

- Growth mindset is more about gaining skills and finding resources to make progress towards goals. How can we better recognize continual progress over time? What additional skills and resources do we need to make progress as a team right now?

- Who do you most admire for their ability to improve their performance? What are some strategies they employed to make this performance improvement happen? Are these strategies you could employ to improve your performance?

- Have you ever done something you believed you could never do? How were you able to accomplish this? What did that experience tell you about your ability to stretch yourself?

- Think about your proudest professional (or personal) accomplishment. Why does this accomplishment come to mind and what strategies did you implement to achieve it? Now consider approaching a current challenge with the same mindset. How would doing this change your thoughts on achieving success?

In my experience, as people we tend to jump from one mindset to the other; it's normal to have moments or situations that bring us back into a fixed way of thinking. The secret to being mostly in a growth mindset mode is about catching ourselves and being acutely aware of how we're thinking. When we share a common language around mindsets as a team, we can support each other in the reframing that's needed to move from fixed to growth. A powerful question to get you and your team started can be as simple as, 'What does a growth mindset look like to us as a team and how can we create more of an environment where this type of mindset will thrive?'

Open communication

Oftentimes, as busy leaders, it can be easy to forget to prioritize one-on-one meetings with direct reports. Leaders need to change how they approach one-on-one meetings with their team and reframe how much value these conversations can add to not only our team relationships but also to the whole organization. One-on-one meetings give employees an opportunity to identify and address blockers, challenges, and issues with their managers as they arise. They also give teams an opportunity to pivot if goals or objectives become outdated, so they can remain agile and adapt as business needs change (Kaboli-Nejad, nd). One-on-one time with your direct reports is dedicated time for you and them. It should be structured, consistent and purposeful. As a leader of a remote team, it's essential to help you:

- Build trusting relationships.
- Stay informed and aligned.
- Provide mutual feedback.
- Identify blind spots – is this person struggling? Demotivated? Burnt out?
- Address topics prone to getting lost in the shuffle, like career development. Keep in mind, for example, that 87 per cent of Millennials value growth and professional development in a job, and one-on-one meetings are the perfect time to discuss personal and professional growth (Adkins and Rigoni, 2016).
- Have a deeper level of listening in remote team environments.
- Improve retention and resolve issues before they become problems.
- Check in on how your team are managing change.
- Build deeper psychological safety.
- Hear concerns or issues that are impacting the team members that you might not have been aware of.

Structured and unstructured one-on-one meetings

There are many ways of running a one-on-one conversation with your remote team members and I invite you to consider just two ways – structured and unstructured. A structured agenda for a one-on-one meeting is used to keep everyone on track and is created in a way that ensures participants check in and discuss key points and updates. It's a conversation that's specific to a certain number of points or subjects. While this type of meeting can be helpful for team meetings, in the one-on-one setting it limits conversations by preventing the direction of the meeting from going to talking points in a natural way. By having a set structure, leaders aren't providing the opportunity for their team members to lead the agenda and discuss relevant points that are important to them to get clarity on. Structured conversations often limit the opportunity to discuss issues around stress, overwhelm and even work–life balance that might naturally arise if given the chance. In this case, it can be helpful for leaders to move updates, information sharing and progress conversations to an asynchronous environment by using project management tools, updates in their messaging platform or even team daily/weekly standups.

Structured one-on-ones offer many benefits, but without a balance of open unstructured conversations, communication can become rigid and not leave much room for ad hoc discussion points that might end up being incredibly important.

The unstructured approach to a one-on-one meeting is looser and can be used at any time. It's more focused on the employee and what agenda will best serve them today. It embodies more of a coaching-style approach, allowing the employee to guide the conversation by focusing on their needs rather than the agenda of the leader. A great way to begin these conversations is by asking a powerful question like, 'What are the most important things we should discuss today?' or 'What do you want to walk away with after this conversation?' This gives the leader a chance to listen to what their team member deems as the highest priority or the most pressing topic or issue on their mind.

Another approach of blending unstructured and structured is to resurface any obstacles that were discussed in previous meetings. Research shows that following up on a problem after the fact promotes more accountability and increases the likelihood of that problem being solved more effectively. For example, 'Two weeks ago we created a plan to help you better create a life-work balance. What updates can you share on that?' You can use coaching techniques to probe deeper if needed, and these techniques are often called for in remote team environments.

Here is a list of best practices that can support you in running more effective one-on-ones with your remote team members:

- At the very least, hold a 45-minute one-on-one every two weeks. If you have time, workloads have increased or the business has gone through a dramatic change, you can increase this to having a one-on-one each week. Generally, 45 minutes to an hour is sufficient.

- Turn video cameras on. You need to see each member of your team remotely so that, in addition to listening to their words, you can also see their body language, facial expressions, and general appearance. For example, have they dressed today? Do they look exhausted? What does their workspace look like? Is it organized and fresh or chaotic and messy? What are you seeing and what are the indicators behind that?

- Turn off every single notification. All that should be on your screen is the call itself. Sure, you might review documents together later but always turn off your Slack, Google Chat, phone and other distractions. If you fail to dedicate the time to your employee, they will fail to connect and open up.

- Always have an agenda included in the calendar. You can use the same one mentioned in the remote-first processes chapter for the recurring meeting and create a no-exceptions rule to update the agenda with any points at least 24 hours before the meeting. You can also include relevant documentation or points ahead of time. This will help you value everyone's time and ensure you get the maximum amount of value out of your one-on-one.

The emotional labour workload for leaders

A study in the scientific journal *Work and Stress* suggests that leaders play a critical role in improving their employees' wellbeing by decreasing emotional exhaustion – a key component of burnout experienced by 77 per cent of US employees (Gregersen et al, 2016). This shows that leaders play a huge role in reducing burnout on their teams and helping their teams feel emotionally healthy and sustained in their work. It's equally as important for organizations to ask how dealing with heightened stress in their teams is actually impacting leaders.

How many organizations are recognizing the particular skill set that's required by leaders when managing and supporting their remote team members? The definition of emotional labour is that of unpaid, invisible work. While invisible, this work is an important part of problem-solving in the workplace, especially when it comes to reducing burnout and stress. Arlie Hochschild (1983) introduced the concept of emotional labour that extended our understanding of work-related challenges beyond physical labour. Hochschild's initial work and hundreds of studies following have confirmed that there is a cost associated with emotional management. For example, a 2011 study involving over 27,000 participants found that emotional labour was directly linked to emotional exhaustion and strain (Hülsheger and Schewe, 2011).

A leader's job today can look very different from how it might have been many years ago and the number of emotion-based responsibilities has increased. For example, in the midst of the 2020/2021 pandemic, leaders weren't just supporting performance and innovation – they also were supporting their teams with mental health challenges, isolation and a global health crisis.

Consider those who take on extra mentoring and counselling of employees in the workplace – surely that is work, albeit unpaid? According to McKinsey & Company's 2021 Women in the Workplace report, 31 per cent of women managers provided emotional support to their direct reports, compared to just 19 per cent of male managers. The report also found that senior-level women leaders were twice as likely as senior-level male leaders to take on this important work. In many companies, this work is in addition to their actual job – and there is no formal recognition for these efforts. What's more startling is that the report states that while 87 per cent of companies think this work is critical, only 25 per cent say it is substantively recognized.

Levelling the emotional labour workload

Organizations today need to recognize the vital skill sets that are needed in leaders that support, coach and promote wellbeing in their teams. What's even more important is that companies take the time to truly understand how leaders are supporting their employees through additional emotional labour activities. Doing so can offer leaders the support that they need when dealing with more emotionally exhausting issues and help them be recognized for this type of work, rather than just the output of their work.

Organizations need to support their leadership teams by offering training to help build the emotional intelligence skill sets that are required to support employee challenges around wellbeing, burnout and stress management. For leaders, it's important to understand what support they themselves have when dealing with these sensitive issues and challenges. For example, who can leaders talk to when they've had a particularly emotionally charged week from supporting team members through various personal/work–life issues? If organizations fail to support their leaders in emotional labour it can lead to stress, depersonalization and other emotional outcomes like lower job satisfaction. There can be higher absenteeism, turnover and work withdrawal, and lower work engagement. Organizations need to understand that it's not just individual contributors who experience the cost of emotional labour; it's also leaders who are usually overseeing and supporting the problems of many individuals – their teams.

Companies should make the necessary effort to understand, disclose and adequately compensate and address the emotional labour demands of the job, particularly in times like these when employees may be even less able to understand what's required of them.

The first step is to seek to understand the emotional labour cost for every team and, of course, it will vary from team to team and is heavily dependent on the industry. For example, a tech company engineering team that's not customer-facing might not experience as high an emotional labour cost as a customer service team that is supporting and solving customer problems and complaints around their banking issues. The customer service team might be actively dealing with frustrated and angry customers on a daily basis – a higher emotional labour cost. The company might decide to not only recognize difficult situations and employees' ability to navigate these highly emotional customer interactions, but they might also choose to offer additional support to managers of the customer service team. Decreasing the workloads of these managers frees up time for them to further support their team members when issues arise. Organizations will also need to look at how they provide managers with additional training and resources that can support them in having meaningful conversations with their teams when they require support.

How leaders can support stressed-out team members

According to the authors of the paper in *Work and Stress* (Gregersen et al, 2016), leaders who focus on providing three specific work 'resources' tend to have the least emotionally exhausted employees:

1 Role clarity: What do you want me to do?

2 Predictability: How is what you want me to do changing from what I was doing before?

3 Meaningfulness of work: Why does it matter?

Role clarity

Supporting team members in being clear on exactly what they need to do and what's expected of them might sound like a basic management 101 practice, but in my experience, it's far too often overlooked. Change in business is inevitable, and when change happens quickly, the team's responsibilities may be slow to catch up. If change does happen in accordance with organizational shifts in focus or pivots, it's up to leaders themselves to help teams understand the what, when and how of the tasks and projects that fall under their responsibilities.

Predictability

The impact of constantly changing environments is not always excit-ing. While some individuals thrive on change and embrace the new, others might feel unsure, exhausted and worried, which can show up as a cynical or resistance mindset. The majority of organizations I've worked with want their team members to embrace change and to not feel that resistance. However, we're all unique, which means that we must recognize that some team members might need additional support and questions answered to navigate change effectively. I am by no means suggesting that we accept behaviours from individuals that are resistant to change and end up slowing the team down (this is a common challenge I've seen over the years) but I am saying that we give these people a chance.

A recent client of mine, a startup tech company, was going through a substantial change in focus. There hadn't been too many shifts in the overall company focus until now; the team had worked towards a certain direction for over a year and were making great progress. However, a brand new opportunity in the market had come up that was so good, the company couldn't possibly miss it. It was one of those opportunities where a decision needed to be made quickly, and a pivot created immediately. It was full of innovation and excitement, and most of the team couldn't wait to get started on the creative work and learning.

Not all of the team members felt this way though. Some were very resistant towards the changes. Now, in some cases, a leader might consider removing this resistance completely to prevent anything slowing the team down when they need to speed up. In this case, however, leaders addressed this resistance immediately and spent time understanding the concerns. By having these one-on-one conversations they could see how different people required different support and answers to help them process this change. For some, it was understanding how it might impact their career development and salary increase plans; for others, it came from a fear of not knowing 'enough' of the new industry to feel capable of doing their jobs. Because of the leaders' approach, employees felt heard, supported and understood. The leadership team identified what they needed to do differently when communicating change in the future and understood that some team members needed additional support on a one-on-one level when going through a pivot.

Meaningfulness of work

Helping our teams connect their day-to-day work to the overall company goals and objectives is not only important in increasing motivation amongst our team members, but it also supports them in feeling part of a team and helps them to see clearly the impact of their work.

Aligning our team's work to their values, the work that excites them and that they can do with ease is helping them to work in their 'zone of genius'. Consider your own role at work – there are probably some tasks and areas of your job that you really love. This type of work gives you energy because you feel capable of it and at the same time it excites you. We all have these feelings towards certain aspects of our job, and we also have tasks that we don't necessarily enjoy. Of course that's part of life, doing and completing tasks that we don't want to, but as a leader, when you understand what excites your team members the most, you can work towards empowering them to be more excited by doing work and projects that they enjoy, are good at, and thrive in.

Below are certain areas leaders can consider to provide a deeper level of clarity amongst remote team members, and thus help them feel more confident in themselves and their work. It can be easy to fall into a trap of doing for the sake of doing without taking the time to understand the impact of our work. When workloads are busy, leaders should intentionally slow conversations down to help teams reflect together on how their work contributes to company growth, culture and impact. When we understand why something is important, we are usually much more committed to it and clear on the task at hand and, therefore, more likely to feel accomplished when we can see how our efforts matter.

Below is a checklist leaders can use to enhance meaningfulness while delegating tasks and managing changes. All of these questions can be used to prompt a two-way conversation with individual team members or even on a team-wide level for specific projects:

1 **Task:** What is the specific task you're delegating? How should it look when this task is effectively completed (use examples if possible)? What should it include and not include?

2 **Importance:** What is the meaningfulness/importance of this task? How does it contribute to company growth and success?

3 **Timeline:** What's the timeline of this task? Is there more than one timeline? If so, what's expected and by when? How does timeliness support meaningfulness or impact?

4 **Prioritization:** How realistic is this timeline, considering other current tasks? Does anything else need to be reprioritized in order to make this happen? In the context of meaningfulness, what takes priority and why?

5 **Communication:** How should the task's progress be communicated on an ongoing basis? What is the process if a blocker arises, or something needs to be clarified? How is effective communication important?

6 **Autonomy:** What are the decisions that need to be made for this task and what level of autonomy does the team member have in making these decisions? For example, do they make a recommendation for decisions and get final approval from the leader? Note that scholars consider autonomy to be a fundamental element of meaningful work (Martela and Reikki, 2018).

There might seem to be many areas for leaders today to focus on but I always advise starting by creating space and time to speak to your team members. This is the most important part of leadership – having the time to chat with your team on a group and individual level. The structures of these conversations often fall into place once this dedicated time is made.

First-time leaders of remote teams

First-time managers, especially in a remote environment, need resources, time and opportunities to develop deeper levels of self-awareness if they want to be able to effectively coach their team. How many leaders have you witnessed failing because they didn't understand how their words/behaviours/actions were impacting their remote team members?

Of course, in remote team environments, managers have all the same responsibilities as office-based leaders, but are we considering the additional skills that leaders who manage virtual teams are required to have? You might be asking the question, is leading a remote team really that different from leading a team where everyone's in the same room? The degree of difference here means that although leaders' responsibilities are technically the same as they would be if they were working in an office team setting, how these responsibilities are carried out requires a different approach. Here are some of the most common examples of how leadership responsibilities change when supporting teams in a virtual environment:

- Not being in physical proximity makes it hard to communicate informally.
- What communication you do have is mediated by technology.
- Relationships and trust with team members can take longer to build when the informal communication that would happen in person is limited remotely.
- The level of trust needed to manage a virtual team is higher, as you can't physically see colleagues and what they're working on.
- It can be more difficult to identify engagement issues when you don't see team members face-to-face every day.

In my experience, it's the more subtle elements of leadership that distinguish good leaders from transformational leaders. Those new to leadership often learn this from their own experiences, training and working closely with other managers. First-time managers usually learn a lot from witnessing other leaders in the organization and how they support and nurture their teams and relationships. Working remotely, first-time managers often can't see how communication is exchanged between other managers and their teams. If organizations fail to create opportunities for newer and more experienced managers to connect around best practices, this leaves new managers with ambiguity as to how to build trust and relationships and how to read communication cues by understanding the 'virtual room'.

In order for first-time managers to truly understand their team, their preferences and their personalities, they first need to understand themselves. Self-awareness is what helps you understand others and how they see you, your temperament, and the way you respond to them in real time. When new managers see themselves clearly, they make better decisions, build more meaningful relationships, and lead others more effectively.

And recent studies show that self-awareness is 'the strongest predictor of overall success'. For example, Cornell's School of Industrial and Labor Relations team studied 72 senior executives at companies with revenues between $50 million and $5 billion (Flaum, 2008). They found that it's not the 'tough guys' who finish first. Instead, leaders with the high self-awareness that forms the basis for solid interpersonal skills deliver better financial results.

In summary, while leaders should focus on their own self-development as well as that of their teams, it's important that managers have support systems that can help them in this journey as a transformational leader. These support systems can include other managers, peers in other organizations, or even an executive coach. Learning from each other's experiences provides a great opportunity for professional growth – a continual guarantee for the leaders of today.

References

Adkins, A and Rigoni, B (2016) Millennials want jobs to be development opportunities, *Gallup Workplace*, 30 June, www.gallup.com/workplace/236438/millennials-jobs-development-opportunities.aspx (archived at https://perma.cc/XA3R-SYE9)

Beck, R and Harter, J (2015) Managers account for 70% of variance in employee engagement. *Gallup Business Journal*, 21 April, https://news.gallup.com/businessjournal/182792/managers-account-variance-employee-engagement.aspx (archived at https://perma.cc/SNC4-F6VQ)

Crossman, A and Lee-Kelley, L (2004) Trust, commitment and team working: The paradox of virtual organizations, *Global Networks: A Journal of Transnational Affairs*, 23 September, 4 (4), pp 375–90, https://onlinelibrary.wiley.com/doi/10.1111/j.1471-0374.2004.00099.x (archived at https://perma.cc/5DQL-EWCN)

Dweck, C S (2007) *Mindset: The new psychology of success*, Ballantine Books, New York

Ferrell, J and Kline, K (2018) Facilitating trust and communication in virtual teams, *People & Strategy Journal*, Spring

Flaum, J P (2008) When it comes to business leadership, nice guys finish first, Green Peak Partners, https://greenpeakpartners.com/wp-content/uploads/2018/09/Green-Peak_Cornell-University-Study_What-predicts-success.pdf (archived at https://perma.cc/44Q2-VKLY)

Gregersen, S, Vincent-Höper, S and Nienhaus, A (2016) Job-related resources, leader–member exchange and well-being – a longitudinal study, *Work & Stress: An International Journal of Work, Health & Organisations*, 28 October, 30 (4), pp 356–73, www.tandfonline.com/doi/abs/10.1080/02678373.2016.1249440 (archived at https://perma.cc/R46W-WSNV)

Hochschild, A R (1983) *The Managed Heart: Commercialization of human feeling*, University of California Press, Berkeley, CA

Hülsheger, U R and Schewe, A F (2011) On the costs and benefits of emotional labor: A meta-analysis of three decades of research, *Journal of Occupational Health Psychology*, 16 July, https://psycnet.apa.org/record/2011-13471-007 (archived at https://perma.cc/C2RG-KG7C)

Kaboli-Nejad, S (nd) How to adapt goals in a time of crisis, *Culture Amp*, www.cultureamp.com/blog/how-to-adapt-goals-in-a-time-of-crisis (archived at https://perma.cc/7HH2-E9V2)

Lee-Kelley, L, Crossman, A and Cannings, A (2004) A social interaction approach to managing the 'invisibles' of virtual teams, *Industrial Management & Data Systems*, 104, (8), pp 650–7, https://doi.org/10.1108/02635570410561636 (archived at https://perma.cc/8NZY-3GCX)

Martela, F and Riekki, T J J (2018) Autonomy, competence, relatedness, and beneficence: A multicultural comparison of the four pathways to meaningful work, *Frontiers in Psychology*, 10 July, www.frontiersin.org/articles/10.3389/fpsyg.2018.01157/full (archived at https://perma.cc/4THL-LJJN)

McKinsey & Company (2021) Women in the workplace, https://wiw-report.s3.amazonaws.com/Women_in_the_Workplace_2021.pdf (archived at https://perma.cc/8BXV-P8UT)

9

Coaching and burnout

As mentioned in the previous chapter, a key element of being a transformational leader is being able to develop emotional intelligence skills first within ourselves. Too often, leaders are trying to support and coach their team members to help them reach their full potential without necessarily doing that for themselves first. As leaders, we have to understand ourselves, our perceptions, beliefs and biases because all of these areas impact our leadership effectiveness.

So how can leaders develop deeper levels of self-awareness? Many companies offer personality profiles and assessments such as the Enneagram and emotional intelligence assessments, which are the starting point for developing this deeper level of awareness. I often see companies investing a good deal of money into personality profiles only to review them once and then put them away in an online folder, never to be seen again. Instead, I recommend leveraging this data to facilitate meaningful coaching conversations on individual and team levels.

For example, ask your management team to set three meaningful goals for their leadership development based on their personality assessment results. The momentum should continue in their one-on-one conversations with their managers. For instance, if they've identified that they need to increase remote interpersonal relationships when problem-solving, they might set a goal to facilitate a team discussion each month simply to problem-solve together as a team.

In coaching these first-time managers (but these questions can be used for all leadership experience levels) you might ask, 'What skills are important for you to develop so that these team discussions are valuable for everyone on the team?'

You might hear answers such as:

- 'I need to ask the team what they think, and listen to their ideas.'

- 'I'll save my ideas until the end of the conversation so that I can listen to what my team has to say.'

- 'I'll ask more open-ended questions.'

- 'I'll be open to everyone's ideas and create a safe environment for them to share.'

From knowing to doing

By coaching your managers to put their new learnings into practice for everyday situations, you're activating a deeper level of self-awareness. The impact of being accountable and actively improving relationships with remote team members will benefit everyone. A Fortune 500 company researched executive coaching and found it produced a 788 per cent ROI (Anderson, nd). They discovered that overall productivity and employee satisfaction were the most positively impacted areas – and those have an impact on customer satisfaction, employee engagement, quality, annualized financial results, and more.

They've not only identified their blind spots, but they've also created steps to move through in an authentic way that will benefit everyone. This is how we move from the 'knowing' into the 'doing'. They might have read about this in their leadership 101 books or listened to it on a recent podcast, but putting it into practice is what makes the difference.

You might choose to ask them a question on this, too, such as, 'By involving more of your team in your problem-solving process, what will that give you? What will that give the team?' A good answer would be, 'It will help you feel less stressed by trying to solve everything yourself, and it will help the team feel more engaged because they feel like their ideas and suggestions matter.'

To support first-time managers, we need to provide them with coaching experiences that empower them to see themselves and situations differently. We need to guide them on moving from the knowledge into the doing, which is essentially what coaching is all about. When we empower them to do that, we coach their teams. The coaching cycle continues.

Coaching through burnout

As we discussed in the previous chapter on the benefits of coaching, as leaders, coaching can support our team members in identifying issues within their professional lives. Coaching also empowers us to look inward and reflect on what changes need to be made in order to work through issues. When our teams experience burnout or high stress levels at work, we can't necessarily try to 'fix' their problems for them. We can empower them for the long term, but change can only happen when there is a level of commitment and accountability from the person making the change. That's where coaching comes in.

While leaders can support employees by referring them to resources or support systems that might be able to help outside of work, there are also a number of strategies leaders can use to help their teams create deeper resilience when working remotely. One of the main strategies is coaching. Coaching seeks to empower the one being coached by helping them navigate to the answers, reflections and guidance that they have within themselves. As covered in the previous chapter, coaching helps build deeper levels of self-awareness. This helps prevent leaders from being the 'fixer' or 'saver' of all problems. Leaders that tend to 'swoop in and save' by offering advice, solutions and strategies may not be supporting their team to be self-sustainable in the long term. Not only that, but because everyone's situation, experiences and needs are different, coaching provides opportunities for individuals to reflect on and create solutions for themselves. Self-created solutions resonate more strongly with the individual and are, therefore, more likely to be effective and actioned.

Below, I outline an example conversation that can support you in coaching your team through stressful issues that are taking a toll on their work.

Leader (L): It's so good to see you today. How have you been since our last conversation?

Employee (E): I've been okay. It's been busy and there are a lot of things going on right now. How have you been?

L: I've been good; thanks for asking! You mentioned it's been busier for you with work right now. How is that impacting you? Tell me more.

E: Well, I've been trying to work towards this project's finish date, telling myself that it'll be less stressful soon, but it doesn't seem to be changing. I'm finding it very difficult to switch off from work and I find myself quite stressed out.

L: Thanks for sharing this with me. When did you start to feel more stressed out than usual?

E: Mmm, I guess it was when these two new projects started back in November.

L: Aside from the two new projects, what else has changed since November for you?

E: I guess I've stopped doing things outside of work during the day. I rarely take breaks now with this new workload, and I'm just feeling like I'm working all the time.

L: What do you need to be able to take more breaks and get back to the healthy way of working you had before these projects?

E: I need support in delegating some of my tasks around project X, specifically the design part of the project. I know we have a new team member who will finish onboarding soon. Would that be an option?

L: We can definitely discuss that with him. So if you were to have all the design parts delegated, how much more time would that give you?

E: Probably that would save me at least a day each week.

L: Great, what would your days look like then?

E: I could take a lunch break, and probably block out my afternoons for deep work so I'd be able to finish at a normal time. It would really make a difference.

L: Okay, so I'll speak with the new team member and discuss taking some of this design work, starting from next week. What are your next steps around prioritizing your wellbeing?

E: I'll start to block out my lunch breaks and commit to finishing work at 5 pm each day.

L: What do you need to do to commit to that finish time? What triggers do you need to remove that cause you to work late into the evening?

E: Well, now that you ask, I just realized I have Slack on my phone, and that prevents me from fully switching off. I've been scrolling all evening. I'm going to remove Slack from my phone.

L: Amazing!

In helping our teams around managing and preventing burnout, coaching is the most effective way to move someone from 'knowing intellectually what they need to do' to embodying more healthy and sustainable ways of working in the long term. Often, when we try to recommend a list of solutions and new tactics to someone who is tired and stressed, the solutions we provide don't resonate. This is because what works for one person might not work for another; we are all different. Instead of providing fixes, coaching helps individuals reflect on their own ideas and solutions and reality-test them out loud in a supportive environment. When we come up with our own ideas and solutions, they are much more applicable to us and our values and thus we are more likely to follow through with aligned action and make a change.

Coaching for greater levels of responsibility

It can be challenging for leaders trying to support their team members with burnout, mental health issues and stress at work. While leaders have a responsibility to support their team members in navigating the complexities of the working environment, it's important to note that most leaders are not trained mental health professionals. This makes it essential for leaders to have access to a range of employee well-being resources and tools to which they can refer their team members should they experience issues outside the leadership scope of responsibility and/or the leader's training and skills.

Coaching immediately creates a culture of interdependence as opposed to one of dependence, which is typically created by traditional management. Coaching is a way of being that stems from a coaching ethos – a belief in the capability, resourcefulness and potential of yourself and others which allows you to focus on strengths, solutions and future success, not weakness or problems of past performance. A coaching style of leadership requires that you connect at the human level, beyond the task – being before doing – and stop thinking that the leader is 'the expert' who has to tell everyone else the best ways to do things.

Self-motivation dwells within the mind of each individual, out of reach of even the chiefest of executives. If people are really going to perform they must be self-motivated. Leaders who adopt a coaching mindset will enable this to happen. For an organization to achieve a truly collaborative culture in which people are self-motivated, there needs to be a belief that every individual is fully capable and resourceful.

Developing your emotional intelligence as a leader

Developing your EQ (emotional intelligence) and the ability to trust is about how you see yourself and others in terms of potential and how you deal with the internal and external obstacles that hinder the full expression of this potential. To coach your team successfully you have to adopt a far more optimistic view than usual of the dormant capability of all people – a coaching mindset. One of the best things you can do for your team is to assist them in not being dependent on you. You can only gain through your team's greater performance and through the satisfaction of watching them and helping them grow.

Your team members must also know that other people believe in them, which means being trusted, encouraged and supported to make their own choices and decisions.

The science of coaching

Coaching allows us to change our belief system and the ways our brains have been programmed, which makes it the ideal framework to support team members who are dealing with issues around workload, time management and even workplace stress and overwhelm. Our belief system is hardwired from years of experience, trauma and interactions with people. In order to change those belief systems, we need to rewire new neural pathways in our brain. A successful coaching outcome depends entirely on the physical changes within our team member's brain. This is called neuroplasticity and requires persistent action repeated over time. With coaching the brain may change structurally by creating new connections between neurons, or it may learn to function differently through the power of coaching.

A recent meta-analysis of research studies looking at how the brains of depressed patients change following psychological therapy is informative (O'Brien, nd). Their findings showed a reduction in amygdala activity (an emotion-processing region), reduced prefrontal activity consistent with a decrease in rumination, and greater anterior cingulate activity, which has a suppressing effect on the amygdala.

Although we might be experiencing the same blockers, the belief system that holds that blocker in place is different for everyone. Unlike most 'one-size-fits-all' training, coaching is personalized to meet individual needs. Research shows that bringing coaching into training programmes leads to positive ROI in many areas. According to the International Coaching Federation (ICF), 86 per cent of organizations saw an improved ROI on their coaching engagements (McCullough, 2022). The same article cites other studies indicating positive ROIs as well as:

- improved executive productivity (reported by 53 per cent of executives);
- improvements in organizational strengths (48 per cent);

- gains in customer service (39 per cent);
- increased retention of executives (32 per cent);
- enhanced direct report/supervisor relationships (>70 per cent);
- improved teamwork (67 per cent);
- improved peer-to-peer working relationships (63 per cent);
- greater job satisfaction (52 per cent).

How to coach remote team members

Now that you have insights into the benefits of coaching, especially in managing and reducing stress and burnout, let's look at how you can start to coach your team members. While there are many frameworks and processes discussing the coaching model, not every leader has the ability to train or even learn all the coaching methodologies out there. In my experience, however, leaders don't have to understand in-depth methodologies in order to coach their team members. They can start coaching at any time with a couple of key best practices and understandings of the process. The best time to start coaching is the next time a team member comes to you with a problem or a blocker, and in starting coaching, I first recommend that you ask for permission.

Asking for permission

Permission means that we are transparent about how we're going to structure the conversation and helps us build a level of safety and trust with a new type of conversation that we're having with our team members. After all, if you've never tried coaching before and usually give advice when your team member has a blocker, we don't want them to feel confused by this new approach. Simply state, 'I'd like to try some coaching with you today to help you navigate and consider this blocker in new ways. Would you be open to that?'

Listen to everything

In remote team settings, it's important to note that coaching conversations should be done in a video call with cameras enabled for both participant and coach so that we can listen to body language as well as the words exchanged. As a leader, you'll want to actively listen to what's being said, and what's been communicated through the unspoken – body language, eye contact, facial expressions and posture. In developing these listening skills, the first step is to be present in all forms of communication and to get out of your own thinking mind. It takes some time to be able to listen presently and attentively in conversations, but when you do, you'll be better able to understand which questions to ask and how to proceed with the conversation and points that arise. It's helpful to create the right environment for coaching, free of interruptions and distractions and your own to-do lists and tasks.

Once you've created the right space that allows you as a leader to be present, and you've clarified the exact problem, the next step is to collect context. Taking the example above, the team member is having trouble managing two projects and the tasks required of them and is struggling with a lot of stress. As a transformational coaching leader, it's now important to collect context as to when these challenges started, how they started, what your team member tried to resolve and where exactly the friction points are.

Having this context not only helps you as a coach understand the root cause of the problem, but it also helps your team members reflect on the root causes for themselves. Using the example above, possibly your team member has an epiphany moment (this is a common result of transformational coaching) and realizes this problem started when they agreed to take on extra responsibilities in relation to one of the project scopes. Since taking on these extra responsibilities, they've found it difficult to deliver their other tasks to a high standard and have found themselves working later each day to try to complete everything that's been delegated to them.

Of course sometimes the realizations can be based on not just the external world but also on the choices the team member made on an individual level or even something that's happening outside of work. As a coaching leader, it's your responsibility to be open to all possibilities in terms of root cases and to rule nothing out. If there are several possible root causes, you can guide your team member in reality-testing each option until they have more clarity as to the most important area to focus on first.

Refrain from fixing

One of the common pitfalls for leaders in the coaching process is that they want to provide their team with the answer. After all, it can sometimes feel easier to say, 'Have you tried this?' or 'Why don't you consider this point?' Sometimes as a leader you may very well feel you're saving time by offering guidance and giving your team members your answer, but you're not. In fact, you're continuing your team members' reliance on you as a leader and you're limiting them in developing their own independence and resourcefulness. While you might want to share your own personal experiences and advice, I recommend for leaders who want to embody a transformational coaching style to save their thoughts and advice until the end of the conversation.

Getting clear on the problem

Once you have permission from your team member to participate in coaching, you'll want to start the conversation by getting clear on what the problem is and what they would like to get out of the conversation with you. Oftentimes this guides team members into a place where they can get clarity on the exact need. It prevents team members from rambling, complaining and talking in circles. Sometimes, it will be very easy for a team member to understand exactly what they need – 'I need more clarity on how to better manage my time with these two new projects.' Or it might be more ambiguous – 'I'm struggling with managing everything right now and I feel overwhelmed. I need help.'

Keep clarifying

For those statements that are more ambiguous, as a coach, it's your duty to keep clarifying with probing questions, until 'struggling with managing everything' becomes clear, structured and specific, like 'struggling with managing the ongoing tasks for project X and project Y.'

A helpful way to continue to clarify these questions is to reflect back your team member's statement and ask them to tell you more. For example, 'You said you were struggling with everything. Tell me about what everything means to you. What does everything involve?'

In this clarifying process, which might be needed throughout the coaching conversation, you're helping your team member not only to think out loud, but also to clarify out loud. In clarifying what exactly the problem is, you'll be much better able to ensure your team member finds a solution that is bespoke to their exact situation.

Move towards solutions

Once you've identified the root cause with your team member, you can start to dive into solution-focused coaching. It can be helpful at this stage to summarize the conversation and the realizations of the conversation so far. For example:

> Okay, so when we started today's conversation you wanted help with managing your workload and from breaking down the current situation, you realized that it's specifically related to project X where you've taken on more responsibility lately. You've realized that by saying yes to more responsibilities like overseeing the full design portion of the project, you'll fall behind on your own tasks, which is causing you to feel stressed out and to work late most evenings. You mentioned that it's not sustainable for you and you're committed to trying to solve this particular issue. So, if we were to reality-test some ideas on how we could solve this, what's the first next step that comes into your mind?'

In helping your team members to brainstorm solutions, you might like to express that there is no right or wrong answer. In the brainstorming process, we'll look at all possible solutions and discuss the pros and cons of each one together. Sometimes, when we move into solutions, our team members might require more time to think about ideas before answering. This is normal and leaders should note that pauses and even silence in conversation aren't necessarily 'bad' signs. In fact, it's actually a sign that your team member is considering something they've never had to consider before.

You might hear an answer like 'I don't know' or 'I'm not sure'. In these cases, it can be helpful for you to guide your team member to a place of reflection on a past experience or event. For example, when they needed to delegate tasks before, what did they do? What worked and, based on that, could they try something similar again?

Moving into the solution part of the conversation might bring up several options. As a coaching leader, you can take each option, reflect it back to your team member and help them reality-test the pros and cons of each option. By the end of the conversation your team member should have a next step to implement or even a couple of action points to take away for themselves.

Closing out the coaching conversation

To close out a coaching conversation, I recommend introducing the reflection summary. Ask your team member to summarize their take-aways from the conversation and recap their next action steps. If applicable, you can introduce timelines for accountability purposes. You may also choose to ask your team members if they would like any additional support from you and when they would like to revisit this conversation and check in on progress. As a leader, it's important for you to follow up and revisit this conversation the next time you have a one-on-one so that you can ensure accountability and progress towards the agreed solution.

> At the end of the conversation, you might still believe it's relevant for you to share insights, advice or experiences and that's absolutely suitable. The main objective of coaching is to help your team members think for themselves first and come up with their own solutions by clarifying their experiences and problems. Your advice and sharing can still be important and valid, but ensuring that you create a balance between coaching and advising is key.

Leadership coaching strategies to promote wellbeing

In an ideal world, leaders would be able to have in-depth coaching conversations about every issue that arises for each of their team members, but unfortunately that's just not realistic for a lot of fast-paced teams. Here are some other strategies to support leaders in bringing in more coaching-style conversations on a more informal basis.

Sharing observations

For leaders who identify changes in their team members' behaviours and personalities, it can be helpful to share observations that can open up conversations that might otherwise be forgotten about in a remote setting. Here are some examples of observational statements that can lead to meaningful conversations:

- 'In the team meeting last week, you seemed more distant than usual.'
- 'I've noticed that you're working at times that aren't usual for you. You sent an email yesterday at 11 pm and, while I appreciate your commitment to your work, I want to check in with why this is. Your wellbeing is most important.'

Asking powerful questions

A powerful question is one that makes your employee think deeply about the future, in a positive, encouraging light. Here are some examples of questions that can support your team members in feeling better within themselves and their wellbeing:

- 'What do you need most right now? What's getting in the way of you attaining that?'
- 'What's one wellbeing habit/activity that has served you in the past that you can leverage right now?'
- 'Considering the change in how you've been feeling lately, what was it that caused the shift in your wellbeing/motivation/energy?'

- 'What are you learning right now that will serve you well, even when things improve?'

Creating momentum

Great coaching conversations prompt employees to define the next steps for themselves and after an in-depth and meaningful conversation, it's important to clarify next steps that can help address the problem. Here are some ways you can summarize the conversation and promote aligned action:

- 'Based on our conversation today, what do you feel is the most important next step and why? How can that support you in resolving the problem we spoke about?'
- 'What is one thing you can do for yourself today that can help you feel better?'
- 'How can we continue to check in on this issue and ensure that you're fully supported moving forward?'

Transitioning into a coaching mindset can take time, especially if leaders are new to coaching. It can feel sometimes like a long way of helping team members find the answers and solutions to their questions and challenges. It's important that leaders understand that the benefits of coaching are a longer-term play. Over time, with continued effort, you'll notice that the culture of your team will change and your team will become much more resourceful and engaged. By bringing all of these skills together in everyday conversations, leaders can prompt their employees to make healthy and restorative choices for themselves and thus create an emotionally healthy team.

References

Anderson, M C (nd) Executive briefing: Case study on the return on investment of executive coaching, https://researchportal.coachfederation.org/Document/Pdf/abstract_681 (archived at https://perma.cc/QD3B-S3VL)

McCullough, C (2022) The ROI of business coaching: Executive coaching ROI statistics (updated), Rhythm Systems, 12 January, www.rhythmsystems.com/blog/the-roi-of-executive-coaching (archived at https://perma.cc/FEP4-Y2FD)

O'Brien, I (nd) How therapy (and coaching) for depression changes the brain, The Neuroscience School, https://neuroscienceschool.com/2018/12/18/how-therapy-and-coaching-for-depression-changes-the-brain (archived at https://perma.cc/WAU7-W7CW)

10

Relationships and recognition

Relationships in a remote team environment are an open concept. As a leader you may have had an office door that you kept open in the afternoons. Your team members knew that when your door was open, it was an unspoken invitation for them to come in and chat with you. When we're working remotely, there is no physical door that signals our availability to chat and connect.

Leaders must find other ways of being approachable in a virtual environment so that their team members can feel supported when issues or challenges arise and know that their leader always has their back – even when they are not physically working together in person. Being an approachable leader in a remote environment comes down to trust, availability and ease of connectedness in a virtual setting.

As we covered previously, trust is continually built upon over time. If a team member approaches you with an issue and you dedicate the time to support them in solving that problem, they'll be much more likely to open up to you, confide in you and reach out to you in the future. Availability can be a challenging area for a lot of leaders who find themselves constantly bombarded and busy with an ever-growing task list. It might be challenging for your team members to find time in your calendar outside their confirmed one-on-one meetings with you. In this case, I recommend leaders dedicate and protect time in their calendars for ad hoc support conversations with their team. They can reflect this time by blocking it off directly in their calendars or creating a calendar booking link using a tool like Calendly. Leaders can then update the team on what their options are should they need support outside of their one-on-ones. This process opens up your availability to your team members, but also helps you protect your own healthy boundaries.

Reflect on the questions below to determine your approachability as a leader in a remote environment:

- Realistically, how approachable are you?
- How can you offer more ways for your colleagues to connect with you?
- How can you create more openness for your colleagues to come to you with questions, feedback and ideas?
- Do you actively listen when someone is talking, or do you allow yourself to be distracted, like checking your smartphone?
- Do you actively participate in company events, groups and parties?

Pre-existing relationships

We know that trust, quality relationships and good connections internally are all elements that contribute to a successful team. However, it's important for organizations to understand how much of their team's relationship-building success is built upon pre-existing relationships that were created in person. This is an extremely important question for companies that have transitioned from an office-based setup to remote working.

The challenge with success built on pre-existing relationships is that, as new people are hired, you'll have two 'types' of team members: those who established relationships in the office, prior to going remote, and those who establish relationships on an entirely remote basis. Gaps between these two groups will start to surface as more and more team members are hired and onboarded virtually.

For many of my clients in 2020, 2021 and 2022, this presented huge challenges for new team members who joined organizations completely remotely. These newer team members didn't have the pre-existing relationships or knowledge around pre-pandemic culture and, as a result, collaboration suffered. While this might immediately pose the question around how we hire remotely at scale, I think we need to dive further into how bringing on new team members remotely impacts existing relationships within our teams.

Think about it like this: your team worked together in an office up until March 2020. You knew each other from working together in person. You shared the inside jokes. You know how certain team members like their coffee. You understand an individual's communication nuances and the way they like to structure their days.

Having a network of relationships enables us to know who to go to when something needs to be fixed or we have a specific question on something. We can rally stakeholders more easily in order to do what needs to be done. Those pre-existing relationships were the foundations of success for many teams when they transitioned to remote working. That means as an organization, we didn't have to focus on team and relationship building as our team already knew each other in depth. When it comes to reducing burnout, relationships are fundamental to our team's ability to reach out and seek support when they experience issues and challenges.

Today that looks very different. How many of your team members have joined your team since you've transitioned to remote working? How is that impacting your team's ability to collaborate, problem-solve and feel connected to a sense of 'team'?

Collaboration questions for leaders

Here are some ways that organizations and leaders alike can support new and pre-existing relationships within their organization:

- **Who are your connectors?**
  Leaders should be empowered to connect team members with other colleagues who can support them. For example, is there an opportunity for two team members to collaborate and learn from each other in relation to a specific project or challenge? Possibly

someone else within your team or organization has a great deal of experience in a particular area or problem. By connecting these stakeholders together, you're helping to bridge a gap, whether that's in knowledge, experience or even awareness around a certain project, task or blocker. By revisiting your responsibilities as a leader and prioritizing activities and skills that empower relationships, team building and collaboration, you can build a more responsible team who lean on each other as much as they lean on you.

- **Transparency around responsibilities**
  I've worked with teams to create profiles for team members that can empower people to know who to speak to and when in order to successfully collaborate and get work done. This information needs to be readily available, documented and constantly updated, falling into the category of knowledge management. We need to strive to get these nuggets of information and wisdom into a written form that new team members can easily access.

- **Problem-solving checklist**
  As leaders, we need to create a standard question to help facilitate collaboration. We have to understand that spending time coaching our newer team members on who they need to connect with and who can support them will pay off in the long term. A simple question like 'Who have you connected with so far in order to try and solve this?' can be powerful enough to promote relationships to the top of everyone's mind.

Here are some other reflection questions that can prompt further clarification on what's already working for your team members in building and creating relationships:

- How can I better connect team members together remotely?

- What habits can support me in promoting engagement within my team?

- What social activities can support my team in building relationships remotely?

Change management

Change management in the remote workplace just takes a little more intentional care. The challenge for leaders today is making sure you have a strategy in place that not only helps people get on board with change but also takes into account what's different about managing change with a remote workforce compared to co-located employees.

Barriers to change

Here are some of the barriers to change that are heightened in a remote team setting:

- **Mindset barriers**
  Positive change requires a mindset for change, and mindsets are powerful things. A mindset can be so deeply anchored that it won't matter how many facts you give someone about the reason for the change or why it's so important – they'll reject it out of hand before ever giving it their full consideration. When you add in the physical distance as well as the disconnection that can come with remote work, it can be even harder to penetrate these mindset barriers. It takes energy and motivation for someone to change their mindset, and if they're feeling one step removed from what's going on, they're probably not going to bother.

- **Communication barriers**
  Communication is critical during any kind of organizational change or business disruption, but even in the best of circumstances, leaders can trip up here. Without the context and connecting points as well as the data and details, people have a tendency to fill in the blanks and decide 'what's really going on' with the change. This can be heightened remotely, when we cannot assess people's body language as much as we would have in a physical environment.

- **Individual barriers**
  One of the biggest issues of managing change is managing the fear of change, which can manifest itself in different ways depending on a person's thinking preferences. Some team members may be

uncomfortable with the ambiguity and emotions created by change and the unknown. Others may fear the lack of security and unpredictability of change. Some may react over-emotionally and tune out the reality, while others may worry about how it's going to constrain them or what it means for their future.

Fear can be heightened remotely for some team members, especially when they are isolated from their colleagues. It's easier for isolated team members to overthink and worry about change, and still not speak up or let their colleagues know their concerns. If leaders are able to understand how they can support their team members through change in advance, they are much better prepared and proactive with any fear, concerns or challenges that might arise, and therefore can ensure team members move through change resistance quickly.

Supporting through change

Teams are much more likely to support change that happens on an organizational level when they can:

- find the benefit in the change;
- aren't surprised by the change;
- can stay grounded and focused;
- have the skills and support they need.

Here are five steps to manage change in your virtual team:

1. DEFINE

It's important to understand the change that's happening and be able to communicate WHY this change is happening. If you as a leader aren't fully grasping the change details, it's likely that you won't be able to clearly communicate this with your team. Understanding the WHY will help your team see the benefit in adapting and help them buy more strongly into making sure the change is effective.

2. CLARIFY

Not all team members will be vocal about their questions and feedback. It's your responsibility to assess the personalities of your team and understand how each member generates clarity with new information. For example, you might decide to run a team meeting explaining the change and follow up with several one-on-one meetings after, because you know some of your team members like to ask more questions in a one-on-one setting. Regardless of how you do this, it's important that you create several ways to clarify understanding on both a team level and an individual level.

Some other ideas for clarifying activities:

- Revisit the change in your recurring one-on-ones with your team.
- Resurface the change and any updates at a team meeting and open the floor for questions and feedback.
- Bring in powerful coaching questions such as:
  - What have been your experiences in navigating this change this week?
  - How can I support you further as we work through this change?
- Send direct messages in your chat platform to check in with your team as to how they are doing with any changes.

3. ESTABLISH

Psychological safety is about creating an environment where your team feels they can speak up, give feedback and ask questions without feeling threatened. Here are some ways you can create psychological safety remotely when it comes to managing change:

- Leave time for questions throughout your communication around change.
- Answer questions by first appreciating them and commenting on the value of the question.
- Take time to answer your team members carefully and, at the end, clarify whether or not their questions were fully answered.

- Share personal experiences of managing change and your own learnings as a leader – this creates deeper trust amongst your team, and seeing that you can be vulnerable will allow them to speak up if they need to.

4. INVEST

Invest the time into continuous communication with your team. Change is a process and that means that the questions, feedback and blockers that might arise can vary through the change journey. Resurfacing the change as you move through it can help you and your team identify potential derailers before they become a problem.

5. RECOGNIZE

Recognition is one of the highest contributors to performance on any team. As a leader, taking the time to recognize HOW your team managed change can help them feel more confident in managing change moving forward. Here are some ways you can recognize your team through change. It's important to recognize people's efforts, not just the result they produce:

- Take time to acknowledge team members who previously resisted change and now embrace it.
- Acknowledge your team's honest feedback and continuous open communication.
- Acknowledge and recognize both on a team level and an individual level and consider various forms of communication – sending a message over chat tools or an email, or on a team call.
- Take time as a team to explore learnings from the change – what went well and what can be improved moving forward.

Recognition is a huge factor in building relationships and trust and is an important part of a leader's job. Let's take a look at how much impact recognition can have within teams and how leaders can create an environment of acknowledgement.

The importance of recognition

Recognition is one of the top contributors to performance on any team, so taking time to recognize team members remotely will not only increase their performance, but when we praise their efforts in addition to the results they produce, we increase the likelihood of them replicating the same effort, if not more, with another task. Recognition can be given as a result of effort, performance, mindset and values.

Issues can arise when recognition isn't part of a team's culture. Over time, a lack of recognition can wear people down, emotionally and mentally impacting them and their motivations, and can lead to burnout. Frederick Herzberg is known for his dual-factor, motivation-hygiene theory, which states that there are certain common characteristics that are associated with workplace satisfaction and dissatisfaction (Herzberg et al, 1963). Herzberg found that satisfaction and dissatisfaction are not on a continuum with one increasing as the other diminishes, but are instead independent of each other, meaning that we need to address dissatisfaction issues and promote areas of satisfaction at the same time.

Motivation factors (satisfaction characteristics) include challenging work, recognition for one's achievements, responsibility, the opportunity to do something meaningful, involvement in decision making, and a sense of importance to the organization. On the other hand, hygiene factors (dissatisfaction characteristics) include salary, work conditions, company policy and administration, supervision, working relationships, status and security.

When it comes to recognition specifically, it has a major impact on the motivations of our team members and also helps us reduce burnout. Research shows that a lack of recognition and rewards is strongly correlated to burnout (Ordever, 2019).

Types of recognition

For leaders to recognize their remote teams in a meaningful way, they must seek to understand what type of recognition each team member prefers. Do you know what kind of recognition your team prefers? Not everyone likes a reward given in front of their peers. Not everyone is motivated by monetary rewards. Here is a list of the most common ways to recognize individuals and teams:

- **Structured recognition:** A more formal approach to recognition, such as employee awards.

- **Unstructured recognition:** A more casual approach to recognition, such as a quick message or verbal acknowledgement.

- **Verbal vs written appreciation:** Verbal recognition compared to sending an email or a chat message.

These types of recognition can come from three main sources: the manager, the organization and peer-to-peer appreciation. Here are some examples of how to improve and promote these three sources of recognition remotely.

ORGANIZATIONAL RECOGNITION

- Consistent organizational recognition strategies, like naming an employee of the month, can be a great way for people to be recognized by senior management.

- Simpler activities that surprise and delight team members, like an extra day off or even a free lunch on a Friday can help teams feel acknowledged and appreciated.

- More formal processes such as employee performance and salary reviews should be carried out on a consistent basis.

- Promoting recognition from senior management executives can really make a difference in an employee's motivation levels.

MANAGER RECOGNITION

- Celebrate milestones and work anniversaries. A simple message can be a quick and effective way to increase recognition.

- Recognize the effort your team members put into their work, not just the results their work generated.

- Be specific when sending recognition by describing the task or accomplishment in detail.
- Reflect on team recognition preferences like 'Which of my team members prefer private recognition?' and 'Which of my team members prefer public recognition?'

PEER-TO-PEER RECOGNITION

- Make recognition amongst team members more formal to help gamify this important habit and make it fun for the team.
- Consider nominating someone each week for a team recognition or even ending the week by sending one person a direct message describing how they've helped and what impact they've made during that week.

So how do we create a culture of recognition within our team? While these strategies are important to explore and try, the key really is to take the time. Recognition provides teams with so many benefits but it's often the first thing that's forgotten about when work environments become busy. Setting reminders and blocking off time for these moments of acknowledgement will ensure that this important part of team building doesn't get forgotten.

References

Herzberg, F, Mausner, B and Snyderman, B B (1993) *The Motivation to Work*, Transaction Publishers, Somerset, NJ

Ordever, R (2019) How to create positive workplace cultures that prevent employee burnout. *REBA Global*, 11 November, https://reba.global/resource/how-to-create-positive-workplace-cultures-that-prevent-employee-burnout.html (archived at https://perma.cc/2AA2-YGST)

11

Leading by example

As we have already noted, leadership plays a major role in reducing or increasing burnout amongst teams. From their culture, processes and leadership mentality, organizations can either be the catalyst for change in creating a sustainable and happy workplace or they can be the primary causes of the negative issues that their team members are experiencing

In my experience working with dozens of organizations to support them in creating more resilient and healthy remote teams, it's always of primary importance to understand the impact that leaders are having on their teams' approach to work. Leadership accounts for up to 70 per cent of employee engagement (Beck and Harter, 2019) so, of course, how a leader shows up in their own remote working habits will have a knock-on effect on their team members.

The term 'lead by example' is often used to describe how leaders should show up in their own work so that they can encourage their team members to do the same. It's a term that's used a lot, but one that isn't often reflected on by organizations. To lead by example means to guide others through your behaviour instead of your words. How leaders act, behave and speak with their remote teams influences how team members will act, behave and speak. Your intention is to inspire others to copy your behaviour.

The opposite of leading by example is to say one thing and do another. Often when I work with teams with this issue, it's usually a leadership team that has concerns and has reached their wits' end in trying to create happier and healthier remote teams. They may have introduced many benefits and wellness programmes within the company, but they find that nothing seems to be working. In these cases, I will always seek to understand how the leaders are showing up in their day-to-day lives. For example, are these leaders overworking themselves? When was the last time they took a lunch break? Are they running from meeting to meeting with little time for deep work? Are they racing through their team one-on-one meetings because they have far too many things on their to-do lists to be present and actively listen?

Your influence as a leader is based, to a large extent, on how people view you at work. Leading by example can be an effective way to promote a healthy team culture. Do you keep your promises? Do you 'practice what you preach' in your virtual leadership? If so, people will look to you as an example of how to thrive at your company.

Communication

As leaders, we want to embody the change we want to see in our teams. Leaders often don't understand the influence that they alone have on being able to create a happier team that isn't affected by highly stressful environments. One of the areas of key influence is how leaders communicate. Communicating remotely is an area for leaders that is on display more than ever. We are so connected through many channels of communication it can be easy for leaders to dip in and out of work conversations or delegate a forgotten task late in the evening. However, what leaders can often forget to consider is the implications that this has on their team members' wellbeing and ability to switch off from work.

Leaders who have team members across multiple time zones and who work on flexible schedules or at different times from one another must ensure that their teams are fully aligned with the work expectations of the team. For example, having a team in a completely opposite time zone means that you'll likely be sending emails and messages outside of their core working hours. Possibly you're pinging them a Slack message when it's 9 pm on their Friday evening. If a leader hasn't opened up the conversation around time zone interferences and established some clear, healthy boundaries on a team level, what do you think might happen?

In most cases, the team members, who want to be seen as proactive and good at their jobs (who doesn't?) will switch back into work mode to answer that question or get back to their leader in an effective and timely manner. If this happens once, twice or even 10 times it might be okay – after all, it might be getting the job done and the team member might be happy with how they're progressing and performing, and so might the leader. But how does this way of leading by example impact a team member's risk of burnout? Leaders who work in this way aren't necessarily doing anything wrong, but they could be unaware of this blind spot and how it's impacting their team's ability to switch off from work.

We can't ignore time zones and, of course, we don't want to prevent people from working certain hours; they are two of the many benefits that remote working provides. However, with increased flexibility and the potential for blurred lines, it's imperative that leaders establish some ground rules to guide how team members and leaders alike will create and respect healthy boundaries. From previous chapters, we know that this is one of the fundamental ways to reduce burnout.

Healthy boundaries

One way teams can do this together is by first understanding their personal working preferences. If I know that my colleague prefers to work late at night for an hour or two because she's more productive at that time, great, but I also understand that there isn't an expectation for me to engage, respond or collaborate with her at that time. For me, she understands that I'm a morning person and I like to review and update my project progress at 7 am before I start my day. She understands, because we had an open conversation about it, that there are no expectations for her to be available at that time for my working preferences.

The second way for teams to prevent this from happening is for leaders to promote healthy boundaries with communication tools and technology. For example, do your team members need to have all of their work applications and emails on their phones as well as their laptops? Probably not. Of course, in some cases your team members might need to be available for anything that's urgent – and I recommend getting clear on what is deemed urgent, because if everything is urgent, nothing is urgent. In situations where teams might need to be available at times outside of standard working or business hours, leaders might decide to call or text. This empowers team members to be able to still have work applications removed from their phones while also being assured that they will be contacted if anything is needed.

Leadership influence

Never underestimate the influence that leaders have on their teams. Influence is made up of their actions, behaviours and choices, and becomes the standard for the overall team. It's important that leaders are aware of how their actions, behaviours and choices can impact their team members and what type of standard they are setting for the environment their team are working in.

Leaders can influence and lead by example around remote team practices like:

- healthy work–life balance;
- taking vacation and time off;
- deep and shallow work;
- healthy work boundaries;
- addressing topics before they become a problem;
- managing expectations.

When leaders are leading by example in a positive way within their remote teams they are:

- taking time fully switched off from work;

- completely logging off from technology when they aren't working;
- taking breaks throughout the workday;
- actively demonstrating what a healthy and realistic workday looks like;
- sharing their best practices and habits that keep them well when working from home;
- offering glimpses into their values outside of just working;
- protecting their time and choosing not to respond when it's appropriate.

What to do when you're struggling as a leader

Leaders are not magically exempt from experiencing heightened levels of stress and overwhelm. Many of the amazing leaders I've worked with in the past have indeed struggled with burnout and stress. In the first section of the book, there are reflection questions that can support you in reducing burnout for yourself, but sometimes, reflections are just not enough.

To create a healthy team, you need to feel healthy yourself. If you want to create clear, realistic timelines and workloads, you have to have this yourself, too. Sometimes, you might have to push back. Sometimes, you might have to manage expectations upwards instead of downwards and that is okay. You will not be able to support your team effectively in reducing stress if stress is being pushed onto you. It's important that, as a leader, you take the time to understand your own boss's success and goals. Then, you can work together to have mutually beneficial conversations and seek to understand each other. It might be the case that your boss or a senior-level leadership team doesn't have direct insight into the challenges of your team. As a leader, you are the spokesperson, the voice of your team, and knowing what to speak to and how to speak to it is a skill worth refining.

One of the essential parts of managing up is understanding your direct manager's most urgent priorities, and then adjusting your own accordingly. If your superiors are putting unrealistic workloads on your team, work together with your manager to find solutions and reprioritize. When you ask for advice, communicate what you've tried, as that provides a context for conversation. In addition, educate your manager on what is positively contributing to team performance and general wellbeing.

Why leaders need a vacation

Taking time fully away from work and embracing vacation time on a regular basis is a huge factor in reducing burnout on remote teams. In the working world today, many companies offer hugely attractive vacation packages; unlimited vacation time is a common perk that many organizations promote when attracting new employees. Regardless of the vacation package that your company offers, it's important to reflect upon how much vacation time is actually used by your workforce. Do most employees use all their vacation time or do you have to constantly remind your team of the vacation days they have left and encourage them to take time away from work?

Taking time off has been shown to reduce stress, promote work–life balance, and improve productivity. Unfortunately, even before the pandemic in 2020, most employees didn't take vacations often enough and over half (55 per cent) didn't use all their allotted paid vacation time (US Travel Association, 2019). However, Covid-19 caused these numbers to plummet even further. During the summer of 2020, 72 per cent of Americans did not take a vacation, 44 per cent did not use any of their paid time off, and 22 per cent took less time off than normal (Holmes, 2020). When asked why, 16 per cent indicated they were concerned they could be at risk of furloughs or layoffs, and 13 per cent felt guilty asking for time off since they were working from home.

The mental blockers to taking a vacation

While there are processes we can create on an organizational level to encourage team members in taking their right to a vacation, we also need to look at the mental blockers that often prevent employees from committing to that much-needed and deserved break. When I coach individuals around this topic, my clients struggle to make the commitment to actually take a vacation. It's like they've got a blocker that's preventing them from booking time off. I hear things like:

- 'I'm trying to "save" my vacation for when I can travel properly.'
- 'I have way too much work to do, and taking a vacation will only cause me stress when I come back to work.'
- 'My co-workers won't survive without me.'
- 'Something major will happen while I'm gone and then I'll be fired because I wasn't there.'
- 'I'm working from home, I don't need to take a proper break.'

These are the answers I hear over and over. This is what the leaders I work with are hearing from their employees AND it's often what they are saying themselves. Of course, it's not just a case of making vacation time mandatory for everyone. Reality-testing these beliefs and assumptions and changing our mindset takes time, effort and, you guessed it, emotional intelligence – one of my favourite topics. What we really need to do for ourselves and our teams is to reality-test the assumptions that we are making. We are reality-testing that inner critic that is telling us we should feel 'guilty' for taking time off from work.

Removing the guilt about taking a break

In the next section, I'll discuss a process that can support you as a leader should you struggle with taking time away from work or need to help your team commit to a break that they really need. The first step is to reality-test the inner critic. The inner critic is also known as the ego – the little voice in our head that tries to keep us safe. It often rears its head with language that promotes self-doubt, guilt and low self-worth. In the workplace, it can tell us things like 'we're not good enough' or 'we're not working hard enough'. This voice usually plays on repeat, singing the same song over and over again. The tape played will usually be very different for each individual. But in this case, the common tape is creating a reason why we should not take that break. The critic is designed to convince you away from the truth and the reality. Take, for example, the tape that says, if I take a vacation, 'My co-workers won't survive without me'.

Ask yourself the following questions:

1 **Is it true?**
   Is it true that your co-workers won't survive without you?

2 **What's the evidence to support that it's absolutely true?**
   Collect all the evidence here. For example, did your coworkers not survive when you took vacation time before? Maybe you're new to the job and haven't taken a vacation yet, so look for evidence of other colleagues taking a vacation. Did their teams not survive without them?

3 **If no evidence is found, what's the new empowering belief that is true?**
   So, you haven't collected any evidence to support your original thought, meaning the belief that your colleagues won't survive without you is false. What is true is that *my colleagues will be absolutely fine without me.*

4 **What's the overwhelming evidence to support your new belief?**
   The evidence to support this is that I've taken many vacations before, and although I might have come back to a busy inbox, my colleagues were still living, breathing, and fully functioning.

You see, our egos want us to feel needed. That's the job of the ego, to keep us playing small, to hold us back and to keep us safe. If we are needed, we are wanted, and who doesn't want to be needed in the work that they do? But we have to link our desire to be needed to our ability to ignore our basic fundamental needs. Are we wanting to be needed so much in our team that we are putting our mental health at risk, or risking burnout? Your job is important. The work you do is important. But here's the permission that maybe you needed to hear: you are not going to be of value and you are not going to perform at your best if you don't rest, replenish, and revive yourself. In other words, take that damn vacation!

There are strategies you can put in place a couple of weeks and even months before your vacation that can empower you to feel more confident in taking that much-needed break. Consider when your organization is at its busiest and at its quietest. Instead of trying to use the quiet time to work on bigger projects, could you take a pause? Some other considerations might be to:

1 Hand over important projects to another team member and use the week or two before your vacation to show them the ropes.

2 If you have important meetings that you feel you need to attend, ask someone on your team to attend instead and take notes. Before you leave for vacation, introduce them to the rest of the meeting attendees and mention that they will be covering your department/ workload while you're out of the office.

3 Of course, you should offer to do the same for your colleague who covers you.

4 Ask a colleague to be your out-of-office email point of contact for urgent matters. Explain what is urgent in your email responder. Pro tip: if everything is urgent, then nothing is urgent.

5 If you're managing a team, give your team members at least one month's notice of your vacation, discuss and remind them in your one-on-ones, and leave an open office booking link the week before should they wish to discuss anything or have any questions.

6 When managing a team, have a main point of contact, a right-hand person who can take the lead on some of your responsibilities. Chances are, they will be delighted with the growth opportunity.

7 You decide if people will need to contact you on your vacation – that's not for me to say. BUT you should reality-test it. For example, a CEO I work with is also solely responsible for the company sales. If he misses a prospective opportunity during his week off, that could cost the company big bucks. So, he trained his head of operations on the standard sales process and gave her his mobile number. It's only to be used once a prospect is qualified. That means he doesn't have to carry the mental load of checking emails and Slack.

Creating healthy boundaries to fully embrace downtime

When you commit to taking a break, you can pat yourself on the back and remember that now your job is to take a successful vacation. Many times I've witnessed colleagues in previous jobs take a break only to log into emails and Slack and ask how everything is going.

Don't be *that* person. Don't be the person who needs to be needed at work in order to feel validated. Spend time with yourself and your people outside of work and get back to the basics of what brings you joy. Your healthy boundaries are fundamental to taking a successful vacation.

For me, it was:

- bringing my dog for a long hike without the need to be back for a meeting;
- sitting on the beach and listening to the birds;
- watching my dog swim in the ocean for the very first time;
- celebrating finding a secret and empty beach for an evening swim;
- listening to a friend talk about her dreams and future plans and being 100 per cent in that moment.

When US workers left an average of 33 per cent of their paid time off on the table last year, will employees actually take their hard-earned vacation days moving forward? Employers need to proactively encourage their employees to take days off and set expectations for the staffing they'll need on occasions such as holiday weekends.

The best way to promote vacation internally is to get your leaders to take a vacation. Yes, to lead by example is fundamental. You can shout 'TAKE A VACATION' from the rooftops of your Zoom rooms but if you have a leadership team that isn't actively taking time off and fully demonstrating that it's possible to really switch off for a period of time, then your efforts will fall flat.

Another idea could be to introduce vacation times as a healthy KPI or OKR. This is a way to celebrate and recognize that success as a company comes from focusing on our wellbeing, health and sustainability. It's about celebrating the 'being' not just the 'doing'. It's saying to your team, 'It's okay to take a holiday, and in fact, it's actually something we promote and we celebrate internally.' A company I recently worked with saw a dramatic decrease in the number of mental health days taken by their teams once they implemented this strategy.

Taking a break and leading by example is such a foundational element of managing and reducing burnout on our teams. If we aren't used to that type of mentality, however, it can take time to truly see the benefits of vacations, downtime and time away from work. One suggestion is to take time to reflect on the benefits of taking a break, after you or your team members have stepped away from work. Do they feel more productive? Energized? How does this impact their ability to do great work? How is it supporting their relationships with colleagues? When we can be clear on the benefits for ourselves and each other, we can see that this work is a fundamental part of embodying a healthy and sustainable team.

References

Beck, R and Harter, J (2015) Managers account for 70% of variance in employee engagement, *Gallup Business Journal*, 21 April, https://news.gallup.com/businessjournal/182792/managers-account-variance-employee-engagement.aspx (archived at https://perma.cc/CG3Y-GWQF)

Holmes, T E (2020) 72% of Americans did not take a summer vacation this year, *ValuePenguin*, 2 September, www.valuepenguin.com/travel/americans-did-not-take-summer-vacation (archived at https://perma.cc/2PDL-L89X)

US Travel Association (2019) Study: A record 768 million U.S. vacation days went unused in '18, opportunity cost in the billions, www.ustravel.org/press/study-record-768-million-us-vacation-days-went-unused-18-opportunity-cost-billions (archived at https://perma.cc/T3CR-S22F)

The Leader: summary

In section three, The Leader, we identified the ways leaders influence, manage, support and reduce burnout within their teams. We looked at the different challenges leaders face today in fulfilling their responsibilities as managers of remote teams and how trust and psychological safety are at the core of having real conversations that lead to the reduction of burnout. We identified how coaching techniques can support leaders in developing more self-awareness and personal responsibility within their teams, especially when it comes to wellness and health. Finally we looked at the importance of recognition, relationships and the power of leading by example. Below are summaries of the key reflection pieces throughout this section which can support your continuous work in reducing team burnout.

Active listening reflections

- How do I actively listen?
- What powerful questions can I ask my team to build more trust?
- How can I set better expectations for my team?
- How and where can delegation support my team members? How might I use it?
- Where might mutual accountability be important for my team?

Psychological safety foundation blocks

- Level the meeting participation field
- Promote active listening
- Make it easy to ask anything
- Address individual working styles

Psychological safety discussion prompts for your team

- What comes to mind when you hear the words *psychological safety*?
- What behaviours do you see in your team that reflect psychological safety? How are these expressed remotely?
- What behaviours may signal that psychological safety is lacking in your team?
- Do you feel that psychological safety is important? What difference does it make in a team, and what have you seen in other teams you've worked with?
- What are your takeaways from this conversation?

Growth and fixed mindset reflection statements and questions for your team

- A growth mindset is more than just being open and flexible. It is also about a dedication to personal development and growth. How are we dedicating ourselves to our own personal growth and to each other?
- A growth mindset is more than only about effort. It is also about process, strategies, focus, perseverance and getting feedback. How can we be more open to celebrating these important attributes as a remote team? How do we recognize feedback as an important element of our success?
- A growth mindset is not about being able to do anything. It is more about gaining skills and finding resources to make progress towards goals. How can we better recognize continual progress over time? What additional skills and resources do we need to make progress as a team right now?
- Who do you most admire for their ability to improve their performance? What are some strategies they employed to make this performance improvement happen? Are these strategies you could employ to improve your performance?

- Have you ever done something you believed you could never do? How were you able to accomplish this? What did that experience tell you about your ability to stretch yourself?

- Think about your proudest professional (or personal) accomplishment. Why does this accomplishment come to mind and what strategies did you implement to achieve it? Now consider approaching this current challenge with the same mindset. How would doing this change your thoughts on achieving success?

One-on-one meeting best practices

- At the very least, a 45-minute one-on-one every two weeks. If you have time, workloads have increased or the business has gone through a dramatic change, you can increase this to having a one-on-one each week. Generally, 45 minutes to an hour is sufficient.

- Turn video cameras on. You need to see your team remotely, and to listen to not just their words but their body language, facial expressions, and to see how they look. For example, have they got dressed? Do they look exhausted? What does their workspace look like? Is it organized and fresh or chaotic and messy? What are you seeing and what are the indicators behind that?

- Turn off every single notification. All that should be on your screen is the call itself. Sure, you might review documents together later but always turn off your Slack, google chat, phone and other distractions. If you fail to dedicate the time to your employee, they will fail to connect and open up.

- Always have an agenda included in the calendar. You can use the same one for the recurring meeting and create a no-exceptions rule to update the agenda with any points at least 24 hours before the meeting. You can also include relevant documentation or points ahead of time. Value everyone's time and ensure you get the maximum amount of value out of your one-on-one.

Supporting stressed team members

- Role clarity: What do you want me to do?
- Predictability: How is what you want me to do changing from what I was doing before?
- Meaningfulness of work: Why does it matter?

Delegation of tasks

1 **Task:** What is the specific task you're delegating? What does an example of this task being effectively completed look like? What should it include and not include?

2 **Timeline:** What's the timeline of this task? Are there a couple of timelines? If so, what's expected and by when?

3 **Prioritization:** How realistic is this timeline based on other current tasks? Does anything else need to be reprioritized in order to make this happen? What takes priority and why?

4 **Communication:** How should the task progress be communicated on an ongoing basis? What is the process if a blocker arises or something needs to be clarified?

5 **Autonomy:** What are the decisions that need to be made for this task and what level of autonomy does the team member have in making these decisions? For example, do they make a recommendation for decisions and get final approval from the leader?

6 **Importance:** What is the importance of this task? How does it contribute to company growth and success?

How to coach your team

- Ask for permission
- Refrain from fixing
- Get clear on the problem

- Keep clarifying
- Listen to everything
- Move towards solutions
- Close out the coaching conversation

Leadership coaching strategies to promote wellbeing amongst your team members

ASKING POWERFUL QUESTIONS

- 'What do you need most right now?'/'What's getting in the way of you attaining that?'
- 'What's one wellbeing habit/activity that has served you in the past that you can leverage right now?'
- 'Considering the change in how you've been feeling lately – what was it that caused the shift in your wellbeing/motivation/energy?'
- 'What are you learning right now that will serve you well, even when things improve?'

CREATING MOMENTUM

- 'Based on our conversation today, what do you feel is the most important next step and why?'
- 'How can that support you in elevating the problem we spoke about?'
- 'What is one thing you can do for yourself today that can help you feel better?'
- 'How can we continue to check in on this issue and ensure that you're supported fully moving forward?'

Your leadership approachability: reflection prompts for leaders

- How approachable are you?
- How can you offer more ways for your colleagues to connect with you?

- How can you create more openness for your colleagues to come to you with questions, feedback and ideas?
- Do you actively listen, or check your smartphone when someone is talking?
- Do you actively participate in company events, groups and parties?

Relationship building reflection prompts for leaders

- How can I better connect team members together remotely?
- What habits can support me in promoting engagement within my team?
- What social activities can support my team in building relationships remotely?

Steps to managing change remotely

1 **Define:** It's important to understand the change that's happening and to be able to communicate WHY this change is happening. If you as a leader aren't fully grasping the change details, it's likely that you won't be able to clearly communicate this with your team. Understanding the WHY will help your team see the benefit in adapting and be much more bought into making sure the change is effective.

2 **Clarify:** Not all team members will be vocal about their questions and feedback. It's your responsibility to assess the personalities of your team and understand how they generate clarity with new information. For example, you might decide to run a team meeting explaining the change along with several one-on-one meetings afterwards because you know some of your team members like to ask more questions in a one-on-one setting. Regardless of how you do this, it's important that you create several ways to clarify understanding on a team level and individual level.

3 **Establish:** Psychological safety is about creating an environment where your team feels they can speak up, give feedback and ask questions without feeling threatened.

4 **Invest:** Invest the time into continuous communication with your team. Change is a process and that means that the questions, feedback and blockers that might arise can vary through the change journey. Resurfacing the change as you move through it can help you and your team identify potential derailers before they become a problem.

5 **Recognize:** Recognition is one of the highest contributors to performance on any team. As a leader, taking the time to recognize HOW your team managed change can help them feel more confident in managing change moving forward.

Recognizing remote teams

ORGANIZATIONAL RECOGNITION

- Consistent organizational recognition strategies like employee of the month can be a great way for people to be recognized top-down.
- Simpler activities that surprise and delight team members like an extra day off or even a free lunch on a Friday can help teams feel acknowledged and appreciated.
- More formal processes such as employee performance and salary reviews should be carried out on a consistent basis.
- Promoting recognition from senior management executives can really make a difference in an employee's motivation levels.

MANAGER RECOGNITION

- Celebrate milestones and work anniversaries. A simple message can be a quick and effective way to increase recognition.
- Recognize the effort your team members put into their work, not just the results their work generated.

- Be specific when giving recognition by describing the task or accomplishment in detail.

- Reflect on team recognition preferences like 'Which of my team members prefer private recognition?' or 'Which of my team members prefer public recognition?'

PEER-TO-PEER RECOGNITION

- Making recognition amongst team members more formal can help gamify this important habit and make it fun amongst the team, whether it is nominating someone each week for a team recognition or even ending the week by sending one person a direct message describing how they've helped and what impact they've made during that week.

LEADING BY EXAMPLE SUGGESTIONS

- Taking time fully switched off from work.
- Completely logging off from technology when not working.
- Taking breaks throughout the workday.
- Actively demonstrating what a healthy and realistic workday looks like.
- Sharing best practices and habits that keep you well when working from home.
- Offering glimpses into your values outside of just working.
- Protecting your time and being unresponsive when you need to be.

REFLECTION PROMPTS TO REMOVE THE FEAR OF TAKING A BREAK/VACATION

1 Is it true?
Is it true that your co-workers won't survive without you?

2 What's the evidence to support that it's absolutely true?
Collect all the evidence here. For example, did your coworkers not survive when you took vacation time before? Maybe you're new to

the job and haven't taken a vacation yet, so look for evidence in other colleagues taking a vacation. Did their teams not survive without them?

3 **If no evidence is found, what's the new empowering belief that is true?**
So, you haven't collected any evidence to support your original thought, meaning the belief that your colleagues won't survive without you is false. What is true is that your colleagues will be absolutely fine without you.

4 **What's the overwhelming evidence to support your new belief?**
The evidence to support this is that you've taken many vacations before, and although you might have come back to a busy inbox, your colleagues were still living, breathing and fully functioning.

Conclusion

In reading this book, I hope you have expanded your insights, knowledge and understanding of burnout in our remote working environments. This book is more than a one-size-fits-all approach, it's a guide, a reflection point and a support in helping you look inwards on your organization and its culture, to truly understand the ways in which your company is impacting and managing burnout. It's also a guide to help you better support yourself, your peers and colleagues in stepping into more healthy, enjoyable and sustainable working habits and practices. Never underestimate the power of making small incremental changes for yourself, your team or your wider organization towards the prevention and management of burnout. It truly takes us to face the problem head-on and be open to many possible root causes to find a workable solution.

What really stood out to me, and continues to, is how organizations choose to manage, handle and solve the problems their employees face when it comes to burnout. While understanding how to manage ourselves, our wellbeing and our own emotional intelligence skills is important in reducing stress and burnout (mine have been even further tested in writing this book), burnout issues are usually never solely a root cause of any one individual's actions.

In many cases, as I've outlined in this book, the reasons for burnout are often blamed on the individual themselves, suggesting that this happened only as a direct result of their actions. We know now that this is rarely the case when it comes to multiple cases of burnout within any one organization.

Of course, this all starts with reframing the conversation with an open mind and a heart-centred approach to strive towards better. I hope that this book will be a catalyst for those conversations.

It's safe to admit that we were wrong. It's safe to say that we want to do better. Not just for our teams today but for the future generations to come. Our workplaces must not continue in this way. If we accept burnout as a normal part of being a working professional, the standard and expectations of individuals' availability and working hours will never really end.

When we look at burnout as a systemic issue within our organizations, we start to get under the hood of the problem; we start to reduce blame and approach these problems with a sense of curiosity, a sense of continuous improvement and learning. That's ultimately what we need to see in our organizations today – an open mind and a commitment to continuous improvement. We need companies to be introspective when a problem arises; after all, isn't that the key for all development? To see a problem, a trigger or a challenge and ask 'What can I do differently?'

When we shift that perspective within our culture, we each feel responsible for the wellbeing of our teams, their stress levels in a professional environment, and ultimately how happy they feel at work. It is not about any one person, leader or department taking all responsibility for reducing and managing burnout – it is a multi-layered issue that requires a multidisciplinary approach and delegation of responsibilities. It's about putting our care for one another as human beings above all else, and knowing that when the people around us are feeling good within themselves, the metrics and the goals will follow.

For me, in putting this book and the research together, I have been blown away by the number of remote workers impacted by burnout, and how it has in itself become an epidemic. I've been shaken to my core and devastated by some of the stories I still continue to hear about how people are treated. I've witnessed thousands of tears from people who continue to suffer at the hands of organizations who just don't care. This was the fuel for my book. This was my stamina. This is the reason I continue to share the truth of this problem, no matter how uncomfortable it makes some people.

It's coming to a point in the workplace where finally employees don't have to just settle for highly stressful, unhappy working environments any longer. While this can be challenging for companies trying their best to retain and attract talent, I truly believe it's forced many organizations to take that introspective approach, which is needed in order to create healthy and sustainable places of work.

Some say that those companies that make office working mandatory won't survive the next decade. My belief is that companies that promote, ignore and treat burnout as an individual problem are the ones that won't survive. It's not necessarily about where we work, it's how we work. It's about how we feel at the end of the work day and week, how work positively or negatively impacts our personal life, health and joy.

We are only as sustainable as an organization as how happy and well our employees feel. The success of our business should include the metric that looks at how happy and well our team feels because after all, we cannot achieve success alone. Success in business doesn't just come from the things we do, it comes from the culture we create and the approaches we take, as teams and as individuals. When cultures create teams of people who feel good in themselves, organizations become unstoppable. Customers are happier, innovation is creative and teams are more productive.

Thank you for being on this journey with me; together, I know we'll make a great impact towards healthier and happier working environments.

INDEX

NB: page numbers in *italic* indicate figures or tables

Printed in the USA
CPSIA information can be obtained
at www.ICGtesting.com
LVHW071551191023
761578LV00017B/327

9 781398 608078